CW00447327

CYNICISM

ANSGAR ALLEN

The MIT Press | Cambridge, Massachusetts | London, England

This book was set in Chaparral Pro by Toppan Best-set Premedia Limited.
Printed and bound in the United States of America.

Library of Congress Cataloging-in-Publication Data

Names: Allen, Ansgar, author.
Title: Cynicism / Ansgar Allen.
Description: Cambridge, MA : MIT Press, 2020. | Series: The MIT Press
  essential knowledge series | Includes bibliographical references and index.
Identifiers: LCCN 2019006326 | ISBN 9780262537889 (pbk. : alk. paper)
Subjects: LCSH: Cynicism.
Classification: LCC B809.5 .A45 2019 | DDC 183/.4—dc23 LC record
  available at https://lccn.loc.gov/2019006326

10   9   8   7   6   5   4   3   2   1

CONTENTS

SERIES FOREWORD

The MIT Press Essential Knowledge series offers accessible, concise, beautifully produced pocket-size books on topics of current interest. Written by leading thinkers, the books in this series deliver expert overviews of subjects that range from the cultural and the historical to the scientific and the technical.

In today's era of instant information gratification, we have ready access to opinions, rationalizations, and superficial descriptions. Much harder to come by is the foundational knowledge that informs a principled understanding of the world. Essential Knowledge books fill that need. Synthesizing specialized subject matter for nonspecialists and engaging critical topics through fundamentals, each of these compact volumes offers readers a point of access to complex ideas.

Bruce Tidor
Professor of Biological Engineering and Computer Science
Massachusetts Institute of Technology

PRELUDE: THE PROBLEM
WITH DEVIANCE

A cynic has a low view of humankind. To be cynical is to regard others with distrust. Contemptuous, if not mocking,
of noncynical natures, the cynic views human sincerity
and integrity with scorn, believing them to be a cover for
self-interest. As a cultural disposition, cynicism foments
distrust, derails progress, and reduces all higher things,
all that is good about humankind, to the level of its own
diminished outlook. It assumes that all human motives
are basically selfish and denies the possibility of a better
world.

There was once a very different form of cynicism—
Cynicism with a capital "C." Its most famous practitioner
was the Cynic Diogenes, born around 412–403 BCE. Diogenes was known for his low opinion of his ancient Greek
contemporaries, but was committed to changing the conditions by which they lived. In this respect, his Cynicism

was the opposite of our own jaded condition where mass cynicism encourages us to believe that any attempts to change the world are doomed to fail before they even begin. This book will compare ancient and modern forms of cynicism in order to better understand the latter. It will explore how each cynicism is the product of and holds a mirror to the society in which it appears. As it compares the two, it will also investigate how one turned into the other, offering a journey through the various intermediate forms that cynicism has taken over the last two and a half thousand years.

At first glance, the differences are indeed stark. As a loosely connected group of mendicant philosophers, the ancient Cynics were easy to identify by their characteristic dress—the famous staff and cloak—their deliberate self-impoverishment, unrefined manners, lack of shame, perplexing behavior, and barking tone. These Cynics criticized the culture in which they found themselves by adopting a way of life designed to scandalize contemporaries, draw out their prejudices, and bear witness to the possibility of a completely different attitude to existence. By contrast, modern cynics are much harder to identify. No longer a philosophy practiced by a tiny minority of converts, cynicism has gone mainstream. We are all cynics now. The modern cynical attitude still casts a suspicious gaze on cultured refinements and rarefied customs, yet its scandalizing impulse functions at a lower key. Operating without social or political conviction, narrowly opportunistic, always on the take, accommodating itself to the status quo it rejects, this attitude has but a sinuous link to its ancient Greek ancestor that refused point blank to accommodate itself to anything or anyone. So when did one become its other? It appears the transition from ancient to modern cynicism did not occur at a specific point in history, nor was that transition absolute. It is marked, nonetheless, by a typographical convention that distinguishes ancient and modern cynicisms by use of a capital "C" for the former, and a lowercase "c" for the latter.[1]

Both ancient and modern C/cynicisms can be understood as deviant—each entails some kind of departure from accepted principles of public and individual conduct. These principles provide the framework within which C/cynic deviance is understood and furnish the rationale by which it is rejected or denounced. C/cynicism is always expressed in relation to some standard or other by which it is judged, and against which its hostility is measured. Both ancient and modern C/cynics cannot abide higher standards—the former more fervently than the latter—where all turgid talk, all pomposity is undercut, or pierced, so that (in Cynic terms) the inflated gut of the idealist can let out a little gas. C/cynics are not "good" people in any conventional sense. Or, in the modern case, and to be more precise, if one is a good person it is *in spite of* rather than because of one's cynicism. These commonalities between ancient and modern C/cynicisms should not be overdrawn, however. Though deviance provides a common theme, it is still construed differently in each context. Whereas ancient Cynicism was willfully abnormal—if it was sick, it was deliberately so—the waywardness of modern cynicism is largely unwilled if not automated.

As an attitude, modern cynicism is deviant in the pathological sense of the word: it afflicts us. This cynicism ranges from the opportunistic and manipulative cynicism of the powerful—who will do anything to secure greater influence and wealth—right through to the abject cynicism of the oppressed and marginalized. The two are bound together, with the cynicism of the powerful giving endless cause to be cynical for those lacking influence, and with the cynicism of the latter leading to a state of indifference or paralysis before the crimes of the former. In these settings there may be good reason to be cynical, but this cynicism will get us nowhere, or so the argument goes. Only hope and concerted political action motivated by a commitment to higher or collective ideals will change things for the better. But still our cynicism returns. It is experienced as a condition we are reduced to in moments of frustration or despair. We excuse our cynicism today as if it were an involuntary outburst, something issuing from a darker part of ourselves that the greater self must resist succumbing to entirely: "I hate to be cynical, but …"

We excuse our cynicism today as if it were an involuntary outburst, something issuing from a darker part of ourselves that the greater self must resist succumbing to entirely: "I hate to be cynical, but ..."

Given all of the above, it is expected that we all have our cynical moments. Widespread, almost inevitable if not endemic, the tendency to cynicism in present-day society is understood by some to be as much a feature of political crisis—the rise of "post-truth" and the "alt-right," the weakening of liberal democracy and progressive politics in the face of populism, the failure of international organizations to respond adequately to global challenges such as climate change—as it is a political or personal choice. One might understand modern cynicism as just one indicator of a broader cultural malaise. It manifests as contemporary polities veer between violent extremism and collective apathy. This cynicism is both a sign and a symptom, perhaps even a cause of dark times. In such contexts, individuals are rarely directly imperiled by their cynical attitudes; rather, the pervasive nature of their cynicism places us all in danger.

Facing this predicament—one where modern cynicism is viewed in such negative terms—it is difficult to understand why anyone would deliberately *opt for cynicism* for reasons other than personal gain, why anyone would commit to cynicism as if it were somehow socially beneficial. It is true that in some social contexts it is necessary to add a dose of cynicism for the sake of appearances, since a lack of due cynicism can be taken as a sign of political naiveté. But as an active choice, the decision to be *more* cynical surely can make sense only as a temporary condition, a coping strategy, a way of letting off steam, a brief suspension of civic and social responsibility that may be enjoyable, funny, even therapeutic in small quantities, but must inevitably be given up as one returns to more serious commitments. This cynicism has nothing to contribute to the betterment of our lot. By all means indulge it in private if it helps you, so long as that indulgence does not impede your noncynical, better nature. Modern cynicism may have its uses, but taken on its own it is thought to have nothing positive to offer.

This negative assessment is the commonsense, nearly unassailable judgment of our age. But cynicism may also be viewed in a more favorable light. To make this argument, it is necessary to spend some time outlining the contrasting philosophy of ancient Cynic deviance, understood as an active preference rather than a regrettable affliction. Ancient Cynic philosophy was committed, politically engaged, and joyfully affirmative, even at its most dissenting, and for that reason offers a very different vision of what C/cynicism might have to contribute—understood now as a positive, life-affirming disposition rather than as a sign of social decay. Ancient Cynic philosophy poses its own interpretive challenges, however. These difficulties tell us a lot about C/cynicism, and are worth setting out in some detail.

Three Problems

First of all, despite its positivity, ancient Cynic philosophy is hostile to the writing of books about Cynicism. From a Cynic point of view, books driven by an inquisitive, scholarly interest—books written by academics in particular—are the product of a taste and temperament, an intellectual disposition that is antithetical to Cynic philosophy. Despite its best intentions, the study of Cynicism will systematically evade the basic teachings of Cynic philosophy and distort those it still has the appetite for.

"Diogenes," such a book might state, "is famous for doing in public what most do behind closed doors, transforming private acts into perverse, brazen performances." Owing to his prominence in the Cynic tradition, it would be difficult for any book on ancient Cynicism to avoid giving some account of Diogenes's most deviant outbursts. But they might nonetheless be considered tastefully. A book such as this might still attempt to ease the reader into the more scandalous aspects of Cynic folklore. Following a lengthy introduction, they would appear only to be subsequently buried by the surrounding text. That text would persuade the reader that the most famous Cynic acts, which also happen to be the most obscene, were expressions of a distinct and venerable philosophy. This account of Cynic deviance would have it in service of a higher cause and thereby excuse or at least make sense of the most shameless examples of Cynic teaching by referring them if not to a greater good, at least to a more serious set of underpinning philosophical commitments.

The book in hand does not take such an approach. Though it offers a scholarly reading of Cynic philosophy, it does not willingly sacrifice Cynicism to the seriousness of such an undertaking. Rather, it returns insistently to the matter of Cynic deviance. It is tempting, indeed, to begin with the most unsettling, willfully perverse examples of Cynic philosophy and avoid all prevarication. Yet whichever way the subject of Cynicism is approached, directly or otherwise, the obscene, confrontational force of Cynicism will be somewhat reduced. The act of writing reduces its impact. Though a book about Cynicism cannot refrain from describing how Diogenes scandalized his fellow Athenians, it is inevitable that any description of him—*as he shat and masturbated in public*—will attenuate the scandal of Diogenes. The moment a presiding intellect gives some account of what Diogenes was up to, it reduces the force of that scandal.

There is a footnote in Freud's *Civilization and Its Discontents* that may help illustrate the problem. Though Freud can be found discussing dogs, not Cynics, the two are related: the word *Cynic* can be derived from the ancient Greek term *kynikos*, meaning dog-like. With this in mind we can read ancient Cynic practice and understand the hostility it invited through Freud's account of why the word *dog* can be used as a term of abuse. Since dogs are also renowned for being faithful companions, the use of the word as a pejorative term would be incomprehensible, Freud argues, were it not for the fact that dogs display two additional, decidedly unforgivable characteristics.

As Freud writes, dogs have "no horror of excrement," nor are they "ashamed of [their] sexual functions."[2] These words could equally well describe the Cynic Diogenes, who displayed exactly those traits. Expressed in public, they constitute an affront to any civilized being, Freud argues, since incitement to cleanliness and order is a key feature of civilized existence, as are the accompanying conventions that regulate interpersonal conduct and channel and inhibit the libido. This explanation of why *dog* is a term of abuse rides on Freud's prior argument that the evolutionary switch to an upright gait resulted in *Homo sapiens*' declining tolerance for bad smells emitting from the posterior. These ancestral traits were not entirely escaped. Clearly we still emit bad smells—*nobody has found a cure for that*—but Freud presents the additional and for him decisive argument: "In spite of all man's developmental advances, he scarcely finds the smell of *his own* excreta repulsive."[3] In Freudian terms, we are still the product of our anality, though we are in denial, of course. Excessive cleanliness and contempt for those who act like dogs serve as symptoms in this Freudian scheme. Dogs and Cynics alike demonstrate how superficial and problematic our civilized accruements must be if a little dirt and obscenity can so easily cause upset.

Whether or not Freud's explanation is accepted, it helps open the problem of Cynic shamelessness to inspection. We might wonder if Cynic obscenity was more than a mere outburst, if it was deliberately intended to draw attention to the arbitrary nature of civilized life and custom. Cynicism invites suspicion of all features of civilized existence. It works toward a reversal in which the finest achievements of civilized living are themselves treated with suspicion, incredulity, even outright contempt. The Cynic invites ire and welcomes disgust so as to redirect it, interrupting its habitual expression and direction of travel. Cynicism causes those it first scandalized to eventually doubt the forces that produced their everyday scorn of all that is lowly and base. In ways that bear analogy to Nietzsche's "great despisers,"[4] a Cynic critique of convention demands a level of objection, an expenditure of effort and a degree of prior training that sets it against, and positions it far beyond the habitual, all-too-easy economies of conventional disdain.

As indicated above, any account or explanation of Cynic deviance—however sympathetic it might be to the intentions of Cynic philosophy—should expect its own well-deserved Cynic reprimand. Within the taken-for-granted customs and attitudes of civilized life that the Cynic attacks are the operations of a self-assured, discerning intellect. That intellect must also be perturbed from a Cynic point of view, where even sympathetic attempts to understand Cynic philosophy cannot be excused from Cynic derision. The very attempt, modeled above, to explain the *modus operandi* of the Cynic should invite the ire of Cynic philosophy. This explanation of Cynic deviance invites contempt not simply because the theory in question, the Freudian theory of human-like animals that no longer sniff one another's behinds, is doubtful. Rather, this appeal to theory is contemptable from a Cynic point of view because the application of Freud, or any other theorist or philosopher to an understanding of Cynic practice, will fail to grasp the significance of ancient Cynicism. The operations of theory are antithetical to the practices of Cynic philosophy. All intellectual activity, all attempts to occupy "higher," more serious realms, only signify distance from Cynic philosophy and failure to appreciate its radicalism. No book about Cynicism will be adequate to its object. The book is an operation of the intellect. It is the medium of the educated, and the educated are the chief group that the Cynic seeks to perturb.

The second major problem for a book such as this one is the gulf—not just temporal, but also in temperament—that lies between ancient Cynicism and its more recent descendant. That distance is considerable, and could even be unbridgeable. One might claim that ancient and modern C/cynicisms are fundamentally different and share a common name only by historical accident, by way of some historical error, a misattribution of the name "Cynic" and its attachment to a more recent social phenomenon that has completely incompatible attributes. Arguing that traces of earlier Cynicisms persist nonetheless— necessarily warped, of course, since the genesis of Cynic tradition is based on a foundational distortion—this book follows these strange traces of earlier Cynicisms in order to reconsider the place and function of modern cynicism in contemporary society. Such an account of the descent from Cynicism to cynicism is necessary to present-day understanding, this book argues, given the fact that modern cynicism is characteristically evasive. This modern attitude keeps its cynicisms relatively quiet as if it were shy of giving them full expression; a position that is at the same time the very condition that allows them to fester and proliferate. Where ancient Cynicism proclaimed its presence in a confrontational and often aggressive manner, modern cynicism prefers to express itself in private, as a grievance.

This reluctance to bring modern cynicism to full expression is considered in the concluding two chapters of this book, which focus on the third and final major problem it seeks to address. Like ancient Cynicism in its nonidealized form, the modern cynical attitude is subject to a robust dismissal. If it warrants study at all, modern cynicism appears as a problem, collective or personal, that requires treatment, whereby individuals and populations

Where ancient Cynicism proclaimed its presence in a confrontational and often aggressive manner, modern cynicism prefers to express itself in private, as a grievance.

are to be rescued from their cynicism by noncynical actors and arguments. This book toys with an alternative point of view, one that is more favorably disposed to the worst traits of contemporary cynicism. Though today's cynicism is potentially dangerous to the extent that it corrodes and risks undermining existing social, political, and economic orders, this does not mean that it is indisputably bad. In concluding, this book argues that cynicism deserves its negative reputation and yet might still be welcomed. There is a productive radicalism within the C/cynic tradition that could be set to work.

This book encounters several problems, then: first, the difficulty and probable impossibility of accounting for ancient Cynicism by modern intellectual means; second, the tremendous gulf that separates modern cynicism from its ancestral philosophy, a gap that no book can ultimately fill; and third, the necessary ease with which both modern and ancient C/cynicisms are differently dismissed. Arguably, any book about Cynicism—and certainly a book of this length—can give a sense of its object only through an act of unavoidable distortion, just as it can give a sense only of what, according to recent scholars, might be key points in the transformation of ancient Cynicism from a brave and deliberately countercultural practice, to an inbuilt and pervasive modern condition. It is written nonetheless with the view that some distortions can be more fruitful than others. To this end, it focuses in particular on the consequences of C/cynicism for the culture of education, with that latter term understood in its broadest sense, ranging from education in its various institutional forms, to the values, conduct, and self-understanding of educated people.[5] As I argue below, although ancient Cynicism did not escape its own surrounding culture of education and traditions of philosophy, it was distinguished by its hostility to both. This point is easily overlooked or downplayed, given that Cynicism ultimately failed in its mission to overturn the culture it attacked. As this book testifies, if ancient Cynicism managed to perturb the cultural hegemony of the Western educated person *at some point* during its self-told inception in ancient Greece, it did not fundamentally derail it. It would appear that the Cynic project to unsettle our educational commitments from within, and thereby open them to interrogation, remains unrealized. Cynicism still has much to teach us—a lesson that begins and perhaps ends with submitting education itself to Cynic derision.[6]

REJECT ALL DISCIPLES: ANCIENT CYNICISM AND FEARLESS SPEECH

Diogenes remains an elusive figure. The most extensive collection of anecdotes relating to Diogenes can be found in Diogenes Laertius's *Lives of Eminent Philosophers* compiled during the third century CE, that is, five centuries after Diogenes, whose life spanned the fourth century BCE.[1] The purposes served by retrospective accounts of Cynic philosophy were many and various. These combined nostalgic attempts to reclaim a lost tradition, with open hostility directed at those who were its "false" inheritors. They include the satires of Lucian in the second century CE, and the critiques of Julian in the fourth. Those historical records that do survive are, then, of questionable accuracy if not outright distortions and falsifications of Cynic philosophy. For these reasons alone, Cynicism continues to evade those who would seek to study it.

Although these are familiar problems for historical scholarship, the situation is complicated further by the distinctly evasive nature of ancient Cynicism. Scholars must also deal with the underpinning hostility of Cynic philosophy to activities that include those of the contemporary researcher. Even if Cynic teachings had been transmitted in a more direct fashion and we could be sure about the accuracy of our sources, Cynicism would be a disruptive presence. As the next two chapters explore, there is something about ancient Cynicism that must defy understanding. Or, to put it more strongly: to the extent that ancient Cynicism retains anything of its former vitality, it will confound its interpreters, evading those who would like to understand where it came from, how it functioned, and what it hoped to achieve. Typically, when faced with a reluctant, decidedly evasive object of research, academic endeavor responds by recommending more of itself, using that reluctance to justify further investigation, piling one question upon another, diversifying its methodologies, inviting discussion and debate, complicating the problem it constructs as it attempts to delve further into the very thing that resists the penetrating gaze, the accounting logic of the researcher. Here, the very obscurity and outward hostility that must necessarily shroud ancient Cynicism functions as a stimulus for contemporary research, ensuring the deferral of the prospect of a more radically upsetting confrontation with ancient Cynicism. The hostility to intellectual culture that is detectable within the Cynic tradition has failed to staunch the activities of research that takes this practice and associated traditions as its object of interest. In recent years, academic monographs and papers dealing with this area of study have followed one another in quick succession, adding considerable nuance to our understanding of Cynicism as a field of study, while characteristically failing to take up the provocation of Cynic philosophy.

Without pretending to side with ancient Cynicism—as if escape from contemporary intellectual culture were that easy—this book calls attention to the tensions one might observe between the culture of education and the radically opposed exploits of Cynic philosophy. Discussions of the educational implications of ancient Cynicism are rare, and those that do exist are narrowly conceived. Indeed, there is a much more straightforward and less challenging interpretation of Cynic educational philosophy than the one offered here. To outline this alternative, it is worth turning to Donald Dudley's influential study of ancient Cynicism, which remains a key reference point for much recent scholarship. It offers a brief consideration of what Dudley calls "Cynic educational theory."[2]

For Dudley, an understanding of the educational implications of Cynic philosophy may be acquired by studying the most obviously educational activities of Diogenes. Here Dudley focuses on Diogenes's purported role as a household tutor, contained in a brief anecdote from Laertius's *Lives*.[3] Though Dudley argues earlier in his book that the story of Diogenes's capture by pirates and subsequent purchase by Xeniades of Corinth (whose sons he would apparently teach) is "an invention,"[4] he nonetheless takes this story to encapsulate Cynic educational philosophy. Dudley presents Diogenes as an ideal pedagogue in this account, with Diogenes paying close attention in his role as Xeniades's slave/teacher to the moral formation of his pupils.[5] The educational program attributed to Diogenes is, as Dudley interprets it, a "compound of various existing systems, interpreted in a Cynic spirit." Here, "ordinary Greek elementary education ... [ranging from athletic training to learning passages by heart] forms its backbone, augmented by features derived from Sparta (hunting) and from the Persian system ... (shooting with the bow, riding)."[6] The emphasis in this anecdote is on the formation of self-sufficient individuals who will go about (to quote the original source) "silent, and not looking about them in the streets." If Diogenes's involvement in producing quiet, orderly pupils does not sound odd enough, we are told that Diogenes's pupils apparently held him in "great regard."[7] This depiction of a Cynic education seems decidedly out of kilter when compared with the more scandalous, confrontational anecdotes of Diogenes found elsewhere in Laertius's collection. As a compiler of anecdotes, Laertius was content to collect contradictory accounts and place them alongside one another, making no attempt to arbitrate between them. Given these considerations, it is worth pondering the educational implications of Cynic philosophy more generally, rather than pick out, prioritize, and interpret occasional and more direct mentions of education in, for example, the anecdotes collected by Laertius. Such an approach—one that reads beyond the story of Diogenes as a household tutor and interprets education itself in broader terms—informs my reading below.[8]

In constructing its overview of ancient Cynicism, this book draws from the considerable scholarship that has emerged in the last three decades, but most of all, it employs the work of two writers—Michel Foucault and Peter Sloterdijk—who were each in their own way unusually attentive and receptive to the deviant, devious intent of ancient Cynicism. Indeed, Peter Sloterdijk's 1983 bestseller, *Critique of Cynical Reason*, and Michel Foucault's last lecture series at the Collège de France delivered in 1984, helped stimulate much of the work referred to above, a research endeavor that offered its own subsequent readings of the significance of ancient Cynicism.[9] If the following analysis appears at times to privilege Foucault's and Sloterdijk's earlier accounts, it is with the purpose of attending more closely to the consequences of Cynicism, viewed here as a countercultural practice, that both Sloterdijk and Foucault displayed some kind of sympathy for.

Although little of early Cynic writing survives—including nothing by Diogenes—some ancient sources do report titles of works that have since been lost to history. These Cynic outputs were said to be rather unconventional, either parodying conventional forms of writing (the satires of Menippus), or subverting convention by adopting nonliterary forms such as the diatribe (associated with Bion of Borysthenes).[10] Cynic writing, where it existed, was also of secondary significance in relation to the lived example of the Cynic. If Diogenes did write—and not all ancient sources confirm this[11]—his attitude to writing is suggested by the following anecdote: to Hegesias, who asked Diogenes to lend him one of his writings, Diogenes replied, "You are a simpleton Hegesias; you do not choose painted figs, but real ones; and yet you pass over the true training and would apply yourself to written rules."[12] Like many other ancient philosophies, Cynic teachings were at first passed on through an oral tradition and taken up as a way of life.[13] Unlike most other philosophies, a subsequent Cynic school was never established, one that might have codified Cynic principles and established a canon. Where other philosophies were only made available in their advanced form to an elect group, Cynicism addressed a broader audience. Cynics were known for their outward behavior, for how they expressed themselves in public, rather than for the distinct and clearly stated teachings of a philosophy in the more conventional sense. The Cynic had scant regard for the formal lectures and exalted language of established philosophy. Diogenes did his best to introduce doubt as to whether he even merited the title "philosopher," inviting others to consider him a fraud.[14] Cynicism of this sort is always on the point of dismissal as "sham philosophy," measuring its success, perhaps, by the extent to which it remains marginal from the point of view of its more respectable cousins. To adopt a base idiom that will define this chapter and the one that follows (since it characterizes Cynic philosophy), one might say that the Cynic "who simply regards such dialogue as hot air—passes wind by way of a critique."[15]

Status as Philosophy

The philosophical status of Cynicism—its place within the canon—is difficult to establish given that it had no fixed *dogmata* and seems to have operated without a defined "end" or "philosophical goal" otherwise known as a *telos*. This sets it apart from other more obviously teleological philosophies such as Stoicism and Epicureanism. Consequently, some have struggled to include Cynicism within the philosophical canon,[16] whereas others have admitted Cynicism only by articulating an intellectual framework on its behalf, associating it with fundamental commitments to freedom, self-mastery, happiness, virtue, cosmopolitanism, and nature.[17] A countervailing view suggests that the most famous tenets of Cynic philosophy "grew out of a continual process of ad hoc improvisation."[18] There were no fundamentals or pregivens. That is the position taken here. On this reading, key Cynic ideas and methods were identified only retrospectively. This process of retrospective reading, which we must now attempt to unpick, would reify Cynicism, rendering it inert, as it marginalized the rebellious impulse, the situated and crafty playfulness, the devious improvisation that distinguished it from all other philosophies. Only once these practices had been secured, interpreted, and codified could they become the hallmark, the inflexible imprint of Cynic tradition. The construction of a Cynic tradition would, in effect, be the death of Cynicism.

Against Plato's conception of the philosopher "as a spectator of time and eternity," one might say that Diogenes was "the philosopher of contingency, of life in the barrel."[19] But even this statement offers too much by way of definition, as if the telos of Cynic philosophy were a life of that sort.[20] According to one version of the story, Diogenes of Sinope ended up living on the street out of necessity. He was not native to Athens but arrived from the borders of the Greek world as an exile, banished from his home city, a wandering migrant who would make himself increasingly unwelcome in his host community. Diogenes is famous for setting up home in a storage jar, but he did so only because the little house he had hoped for could not be arranged in time.[21] The barrel—in which he would not just live but roll about—gains significance later, as the site of his more deviant, devious Cynicism: unprincipled and doggedly subversive.

If Cynic philosophy was improvised and contingent, and did not begin with a dogma or declaration of what it valued most, its development and developing form should be understood as a function of its context. Those still searching for definition, for some clear, canonical statement concerning the nature and intent of Cynicism might, then, opt for the opposite approach, and define Cynic philosophy by what it opposed. But here, again, Cynicism wrong-foots its interpreters; Cynicism was not reactive in any straightforward sense. A Cynic does not simply oppose, and define Cynic philosophy in reaction to what is valued or given esteem. Despite appearances, Cynics had nothing against the pursuit of virtue, for example, which is to say, they had no *principled* philosophical objections to virtue as such. Their contempt was heaped on the idea that virtue must be based on canonical principles and should be cultivated in a rarefied atmosphere. For this they would famously be accused of attempting a "shortcut to virtue," for undermining a set of pedagogic assumptions that underpin Western philosophy and its educational and religious legacies. As Seneca (first-century Roman statesman and tutor to the emperor Nero) put it, "Virtue only comes to a character which has been thoroughly schooled and trained and brought to a pitch of perfection by unremitting practice."[22] Virtue is the possession of the wise, well versed, and well off; the exclusivity of virtue, Seneca writes, is "the best thing about her." There is, he continues, "about wisdom [and the virtue it cultivates] a nobility and magnificence in the fact that she ... is not a blessing given to all and sundry."[23] Without defining the Cynic attitude by its negation, this foundational conceit of the educated person was clearly worth undermining from a Cynic point of view.

The Cynic was not straightforwardly anticulture, either. Here it is worth sounding a broader note of caution to avoid simplifying the object of Cynic countercultural critique. Insofar as street Cynics later opposed the *paideia*, or learned culture of a Roman philosopher-emperor such as Julian, they were confronted with a cultural phenomenon that was complex and ambiguous in its operations. As Peter Brown argues, *paideia* should not be understood simply as a system of exclusion by which the Roman nobility and political elite asserted their "exalted" status as bearers of culture and refinement. If that were the case, the task for Cynics would be relatively straightforward; all Cynic practice would need to do is reveal *paideia* as an artifice, a set of arbitrary cultural values by which the nobility exalts itself on false pretense. Cynics could then attack *paideia* as an agent of cultural oppression. But as a marker of nobility and system of decorum, *paideia* did not just exalt the powerful. In Brown's analysis, "it controlled them by ritualizing their responses and by bridling their raw nature through measured gestures."[24] Its rituals helped regulate the violence of imperial power, submitting it to convention, rendering it predictable. Its aristocratic protocols operated against "a tide of horror that lapped close to the feet of educated persons."[25] Consequently, or so one might conclude, the task of the Cynic cannot be to destroy the pretensions of culture and leave it there, since that would open the way to unbridled imperial power. Cynicism, from this point of view, is not just anticulture; it attempts a more exacting critique of the systems of power that culture is imbricated with and supportive of.

Fearless Speech

The hostility to intellectual culture found in Cynic philosophy should also not be essentialized, as if Cynics were just a bunch of anti-intellectuals with an axe to grind. Cynics were not hostile to attempts to understand the world in which they lived. They were merely suspicious of the common prejudice that the world can be adequately understood only by adopting the conventions of rationality endorsed by a particular philosophical school (or in contemporary terms, the idea that the intellect must adhere to a particular discipline, method, or mode of writing and speech). As a philosopher of contingency, the Cynic is said to live without certainties and does not mourn their absence. The Cynic's life could be described as an experiment, determined to perturb and explore the boundaries of ordinary existence. It is in this sense that Cynic philosophy constitutes "a dialogue with the contingencies that shape the material conditions of existence"—as has been argued.[26] Indeed, to switch for a moment to the work of Mikhail Bakhtin, Diogenes can be approached as an early player in a wider (and much longer) revolution that would place immediate context and experiment at the center of literary forms that otherwise prioritized the relatively fixed parameters of tradition. As Bakhtin interprets, the unpredictable and open-ended engagements of "unofficial thought"—represented most notably by the Cynics—were beginning to contest everything with "an official air," with its distant gaze, and determination to ignore low culture in favor of its own, unimpeachable hierarchy of values.[27] For Diogenes, this experiment often takes the form of a hostile engagement, where the philosopher sends out provocations, examines the retorts provoked by them, and comes to understand the limits these retorts reflect. The challenge is to improvise a way of life that can sustain itself alongside and outside these limits. By rejecting the consolations and comfortable illusions of intellectual culture, by risking social marginalization, alienation, and political retribution, by actively seeking destitution and physical hardship, the Cynic discovered the world through a series of practical confrontations with it.

The most famous anecdote of Cynic provocation before the forces of officialdom is the story of Diogenes's exchange with Alexander the Great: "When he was sunning himself ... Alexander came and stood over him and said: 'Ask me for anything you want.' To which he replied, 'Stand out of my light.'"[28] This anecdote has been subject to many different readings. It has been taken as an example of Cynic integrity before power, of its commitment to poverty in the face of considerable temptation—a sign of divine virtue in its Christianized interpretation[29]—or as a demonstration of the philosophical independence and higher sovereignty of Cynic philosophy, a status that even Alexander recognized according to another anecdote from Laertius's *Lives*: "Alexander is reported to have said, 'Had I not been Alexander, I should have liked to be Diogenes.'"[30] This anecdote might be further understood as offering an example of Cynic commitment to critique, if not protest before power—where Diogenes spoke "truth to power" consistently and unflinchingly. We might take Diogenes as a model protestor in this respect and conclude that contemporary cynicism should—if it can learn anything from its ancient ancestor—learn this: speak truth to power in all circumstances, do not revere the powerful, do not tone down your language when put to the test. And yet, this could be a mistaken view (though it is not an uncommon one), since the anecdote speaks for Alexander as much as it does for Diogenes. It speaks of his clemency, his wisdom before this decidedly rude representative of philosophy. It shows that Alexander (who was Aristotle's pupil) can still be touched by the call of philosophy. This anecdote also risks downplaying the situated craftiness of Cynic philosophy, which was certainly brash, and definitely courageous, but did not reduce itself to commandments such as one might find represented here, namely, the notion that a good Cynic will always speak truth to power.

Fearless speech, otherwise known as *parrhesia*, has nonetheless become a recurring theme in accounts of Cynic philosophy. It is prominent in Foucault's interpretation.[31] As a Cynic theme it draws attention to the audacity of the Cynic philosopher who speaks freely, though the term applies to others, too, most notably Socrates, who conducted free speech as dialogue. The term recurs throughout Greek and Roman literature, describing a mode of interaction in which free men might indulge (given their oppressed status, women, slaves, outsiders, and children were debarred from taking part in parrhesiastic exchanges). Though parrhesia clearly took different forms in antiquity, Cynicism stretched its basic definition in terms of who might partake, while pushing this mode of speech toward its limit, a point at which free speech ceases to be tolerated, and dialogue is replaced by violent reprisal. Since freedom to practice parrhesia was generally associated with "the rights of a citizen (in a democratic state) or the privileges of an aristocrat," it is argued that Diogenes's claim to parrhesia, issuing as it did from the "bottom of the social hierarchy—as an impoverished noncitizen"—was a bold maneuver.[32] Parrhesia was remodeled by removing it from an elite context governed by conventions of decorum and putting it to use within a setting that refused these restraints and should not have been practicing parrhesia in the first place.

Cynicism distorted the basic nature of parrhesia in other respects too. Parrhesia depended on an agreement between interlocutors to bear the other's free speech without reprisal. Cynic philosophy stretched this agreement to breaking point. In basing its use of parrhesia so heavily on the form of an insult (rather than the form of an uncomfortable truth that the parrhesiast is trying, valiantly but respectfully, to put across), the Cynic parrhesiast plays "at the very limits of the parrhesiastic contract," as Foucault puts it.[33] Unlike Socrates—who in many respects represents the ideal Western educator[34]—a Cynic such as Diogenes of Sinope would not be so courteous as to engage in respectful dialogue, in the drawn-out, carefully regulated sense of that word, where mutual interaction depends at least on a pretense of mutual regard. Diogenes's speech poured forth heedless of whether or not one consented to its onslaught. This required courage, though of a different sort. While Socrates risks the irritation if not anger of his companions by persuading them through dialogue, trickery, and irony of their ignorance, of not knowing what they claimed to know, the Cynic risks the vengeance of his auditors more openly, berating them to reject and despise everything they accept to be true and proper. Whereas the Socratic teacher "plays with his interlocutor's ignorance" to generate a thirst for wisdom, so as to cause them to apply themselves more earnestly and thoroughly to their education, Diogenes seeks to hurt their *pride*.[35] Dialogue is replaced by diatribe and insult, or it is suspended altogether, whereupon the Cynic exhibits him- or herself shamelessly before a public, causing deliberate offense. While Socratic irony seeks to create a sense of existential doubt among friends and acquaintances, the Cynic gives cause to riot.

The Cynic speaks fearlessly only after becoming, or so as to become, free of attachments. The Cynic must attempt to become free of duties that function as constraints. Foremost among these constraints are the operations of the conscience, a tool of self-government, which, as Foucault argues, was perfected during the long interval of Christendom and bequeathed upon modernity to become the key means by which its modern and late-modern inheritors are constrained.[36] Again, a word of caution is necessary. To suggest that the Cynic seeks to become free of these chattels might give the impression that the perfect Cynic would be a kind of sociopath; bold, disinhibited, free of remorse, this character would be at liberty to pursue his or

While Socratic irony
seeks to create a sense
of existential doubt
among friends and
acquaintances, the Cynic
gives cause to riot.

her philosophy of deviance without hindrance. Cynic philosophy was, however, far more imbricated in and appreciative of the social norms it set out to question than this depiction of the Cynic as a kind of sociopath would allow. The Cynic is committed to the complex unraveling of social norms. Cynic philosophy was not modeled on the idea of straightforward escape as if it were a matter of breaking loose, stepping outside, or turning one's back on convention. For the Cynic, escapees always carry more baggage than they realize.

Impoverishment

The difficulty of escape is exemplified by the practice of Cynic impoverishment. This activity demonstrates that the pursuit of freedom, a life free of attachments, has paradoxical effects. The Cynic begins by stripping down existence, getting rid of anything that might be considered superfluous, casting off material goods that would tie the Cynic down through his or her dependence on them. In a notorious anecdote, Diogenes even threw away his wooden cup, which was said to be one of his last belongings. Having observed a boy drink from his hollowed hand, Diogenes found his cup to be yet another unnecessary burden.[37] As Foucault interprets, the Cynic of this more radical persuasion was "always looking for possible further destitution." Cynic poverty was a "dissatisfied poverty which strives to get back to the ground of the absolutely indispensable." It was an "indefinite poverty endlessly at work on itself."[38] This deliberate and progressive impoverishment committed the Cynic to a life of dirt and dishevelment, affording an independence of sorts—liberation from the trappings of wealth and civilized society— though the pursuit of impoverishment also tied the Cynic to his (and sometimes her) materially advantaged superiors. It imposed a vicious dependence of its own, as the Cynic became increasingly reliant on the alms of others. The stigma this entailed should not be underestimated given the social context, where personal honor ranked so highly as a virtue among "free" men. To court dishonor in such a way was a radical test of the Cynic's resolve to live a different life. It also ensured that Cynic poverty was more than a romantic affectation; the Cynic deliberately seeks the shame of penury. Presumably those who overcome the worst humiliation will achieve the most thorough purging of all false codes of conduct and notions of decency. The route to independence, rather oddly, then, is through the Cynic's insufferable dependence on the charity of others. To enhance the effect, the Cynic must learn to be resolutely ungrateful when given alms and to be indifferent to those who pass judgement. One portrait depicts Demetrius, a first-century Cynic from Corinth, refusing money from the Roman Emperor. "If he wanted to tempt me, he should have offered me the whole Empire," the Cynic responds.[39]

The Body Educator

Cynicism deliberately upset the conventions of philosophy and the pedagogical relationships it depended upon. To this might be added the further suggestion, itself a little scandalous, that Cynics brought the underpinning aggression of Western education to the surface by basing their educational relationships on the form of an insult (a point to which I return in chapter 3). In doing so, Cynics placed the body firmly at the center of their teaching practice. As an educational activity, and by contrast to the stiff austerity of Platonism, Cynic philosophy is rooted in the experience of the body, which it embraces as essentially ungovernable. The body betrays us precisely when we wish it would submit. Contrast this with Plato's dialogue the *Phaedo*, in which the body is conceptualized as a distracting source of "loves and desires and fears and all sorts of fancies and a great deal of nonsense, with the result that we literally never get an opportunity to think at all about anything." So long as we remain adversely affected by it, Plato continues, "there is no chance of our ever attaining satisfactorily to our object, which we assert to be Truth."[40] For the Cynic, the body operates very

Cynic philosophy is rooted in the experience of the body, which it embraces as essentially ungovernable.

differently, in relation to a radically altered understanding of truth and how it is to be produced. Cynic truth appears as a product of scandal, as a "scandal of the truth," in Michel Foucault's words, an event that is mediated by the body and its emissions.[41] This scandal helps question educational regimes that submit to restrictive conceptions of truth or wisdom based on a promise of realization and fulfillment that is forever withheld. The Cynic notes how this educational promise is itself attached to a demand, a call to domesticate the body in anticipation, and by way of preparation for a promise that is never delivered. By explicit contrast, where the unrestrained, immediate, and laughable presence of Cynic truth appears, "the very body of the truth is made visible."[42] Cynic truth appears in a style of life that undermines the abstract seriousness of conventional truth, with its claims to improvement, and its persistent deferrals.

Cynic truth is indexed to the Cynic body, which bears witness to reality, bringing to question the value of so-called higher things and the demands they make upon us. Where Plato sought to "define the soul's being in its radical separation" from the life of the body, the Cynic operates in the opposite direction, seeking to reduce "life to itself, to what it is in truth." As Foucault interprets, this basic truth is revealed through the very act of living as a Cynic, where the Cynic does not simply cast aside his or her last possessions (with the exception of the famous cloak and staff). Rather, "all pointless conventions and all superfluous opinions" are to be given up, in a "general stripping of existence."[43]

In each case, the "true life" takes a different form. For Plato it is associated with the life that is simple, the life that does not conceal its intentions, is straight, undeviating, and oriented to a higher order. This philosophical life is set against the life of those who still fall "prey to the multiplicity of [their] desires, appetites, and impulses."[44] The true life is evaluated by its adherence to rules of good conduct (which Plato and his inheritors outline), but more than this, by its overall (apparent) unity. It is the life that remains unchanged in the face of adversity.[45] This higher existence is achieved by those few who have the strength and discipline to maintain a secure and stable identity amid corruption and upheaval. It is the life of an incipient educated elite, of those who justify their elevation above the uneducated, uncultivated masses in near cosmic terms. As such, it becomes the object of desire of philosopher emperors and statesmen such as Marcus Aurelius, Seneca, and Julian. With adjustment it will form the underpinning assumption of a nineteenth-century liberal education and its masculine ideal, the liberal "gentleman," which, shorn of its more obvious elitism, still influences us to this day in the guise of the educated person who espouses virtues of moderation and constancy from positions of relative comfort.

This was a considerable edifice to oppose, and remains so, even in its watered-down, contemporary secular manifestation—the educated person who values people of "substance," taste, and cultivated intellect above those without. For the Cynic, the "true life" operates completely differently. It is the dog's life. Diogenes was known as the "dog" and responded in kind: "At a dinner some people were tossing bones to him as though he were a dog." So Diogenes "rid himself of them by pissing on them."[46] Diogenes remained true to his philosophy in this sense, doing in public what others conceal. He extended if not radicalized Plato's injunction to be unflagging in one's commitment to truth and remain unchanged in the face of adversity. By acting the part of the dog, Diogenes inverted the humiliation intended for him. He embraced his caricature, injuring the dignity of those he pissed on, acting without modesty or shame.

DEFACE THE CURRENCY: ANCIENT CYNICISM BEYOND THE PALE

From the perspective of civilized society, dogs should be toilet trained. They must be subjected to the will of their master as they learn to master themselves. For the Greek philosopher, mastery always begins at home; the "true life" is interpreted as a *sovereign life* in which the philosopher achieves, or at least works toward, self-mastery. This life is "sovereign" insofar as it attempts a high degree of self-control, submitting the faculties of mind and body to the will of the intellect. No part of the philosopher's self thus imagined should escape the discipline and composure of a well-governed mind.

This kind of self-possession is not only the high ideal to which Plato's philosopher king aspires. It is also the Roman Stoic dream of a figure such as Seneca. According to this distinctly masculine conception of philosophy, it is believed that the sovereign life will be beneficial to others.[1] Indeed, the generosity of the sovereign life is constructed as if it were an obligatory, necessary component of that existence. The philosopher provides students and friends alike with assistance and direction, extending the same care of self (a form of diligent self-denial) that has resulted in the philosopher's self-mastery, to the care of the student or friend. There will be wider benefits too, since the philosopher's life offers a lesson that is of greater, if not universal significance. The splendor and brilliance of the sovereign life, the life of complete self-mastery, "adorns humankind"[2] from this point of view, and educates it too, having an influence so profoundly far reaching it continues long after the philosopher's exemplary life has ended.

Such ideas have maintained their dominance; they recur, for instance, in the nineteenth-century revival of liberal education, and at a lower level, in the development of popular schooling that was based in part on the notion that teachers would act like secular priests, serving as moral exemplars to be emulated by the offspring of the poor.[3] Such ideas may also be found in the argument for a modern humanities curriculum, which claims that people of culture and refinement are necessary to bear society through periods of fragmentation, where no era has faced so much difficulty as the modern period.[4] It remains the case that "the security of the humanities within institutions of higher education in particular rests on the continuing assumption that they are intrinsically support-ive of 'civilization'—that is, of the Establishment."[5] It is not necessary to be a Cynic to point out the long-standing discrepancy between this ideal and the reality of educa-tional practice. But the Cynic takes the argument further, gesturing to a rival mode of existence that runs counter to the beneficent humanism of a liberal education.

Like the true life, the idea of a sovereign existence is hijacked and undermined in a characteristic gesture of Cynic détournement. The very idea of sovereignty is inverted and dirtied. The Cynic also claims to be liv-ing a sovereign existence, to be a "king" among men, but adopts the mantle of a sovereign existence only to bring it down to earth. This philosopher has achieved "sovereign" self-composure rather differently. To develop a point in-troduced in the preceding chapter, the Cynic chooses to pursue destitution, "pushing back the limits of what he [or she] can bear"[6] in order to develop a completely different way of relating to the world. This "sovereign" life still en-tails a duty to others, what a liberal-minded thinker might call a duty of care. The Cynic life involves a dedication to others that operates without gratitude or recognition. The Cynic does not offer a beautiful example for others to emu-late. The Cynic life does not adorn humankind. The Cynic existence is committed to a personal and public disfigure-ment of what is valued most in this idea, this notion of our common humanity. The Cynic still adopts the role of public benefactor, but Cynic generosity is self-consciously and deliberately harsh. In words attributed to Diogenes: "Other dogs bite their enemies, but I my friends, so as to save them."[7]

Aggressive Teaching

With this conception of the Cynic in mind, Foucault describes the Cynic as an "aggressive benefactor, whose main instrument is, of course, the famous diatribe." The Cynic "speaks out and attacks"; there is something deliberately, openly violent about Cynic philosophy.[8] Nonetheless, portraying Cynic philosophy in this way—as a philosophy that benefits others by inflicting violence upon them— risks presenting Cynics as straightforward aggressors, though Diogenes would charm others, flatter them even. This ability to switch between aggression and charm provides another example of Cynic flexibility. It offers further evidence of the militant suppleness of a way of life designed to negotiate and unpick social relations, confusing or wrong-footing the Cynic's interlocutor, encouraging pride and good feeling if only to "prepare the way for [and enhance the effect of] additional aggressive exchanges."[9] As first-century notable and rhetorician Dio Chrysostom explains, Diogenes would use honeyed words, "just as nurses, after giving the children a whipping, tell them a story to comfort and please them."[10] Undue focus on Cynic aggression also risks downplaying or distracting from the more easily disguised—because apparently benign—violence of other breeds of benefaction.[11] It implies by contrast that the generosity of other schools of ancient philosophy, where philosophers were conceived as physicians of the soul, was a generosity without aggression. This reflects how those schools presented themselves, where the violence of philosophy is reconfigured as necessary discomfort, a type of pain that is apparently needed for the reorientation of the soul. From the perspective of respectable philosophy, it makes as much sense to describe the philosopher who cares for the soul as aggressive as it does to describe the doctor who administers surgery as a perpetrator of violence. However, such justification of the role of philosophy, of its intrusion upon the soul as care for the soul, holds only so long as the philosophy of the practitioner is held in regard. And this is where Cynicism intervenes. By drawing attention to the violence of its own philosophy, and by holding all rivals in such low esteem, Cynicism points out that if we are able to doubt the philosophy, we must be able to see its aggression. Cynicism makes the point that the philosopher who gives kindly advice, who perhaps "adorns" humankind with the beautiful example of his presence, is also aggressive in promoting his version of the good. The Cynic is unique only for openly declaring his or her aggressive intent.

In its educational engagements, Cynicism embraces quite explicitly "the form of a battle"[12] or war, "with peaks of great aggressivity and moments of peaceful calm."[13] For Platonists and Stoics, the battle is largely covered over with refinement, with the avowed sophistication of respectable philosophy, but it is a battle nonetheless. It takes form as a fight against passions, vices, desires, and false appetites, as a philosopher seeks "the victory of reason over his own appetites or his soul over his body."[14] Some version of the philosopher's fight, along with its recommended destination, is then prescribed for others.

The Cynics also battled with passions and appetites, and in that respect were not so very distant from their more respectable philosopher-contemporaries; only this battle was extended to "customs, conventions, institutions, laws, and a whole condition of humanity." It was a battle against vices, though these were approached not as individual flaws, but as "vices which afflict humankind as a whole, the vices of men," as Foucault puts it; vices "which take shape, rely upon, or are at the root of their customs, ways of doing things, laws, political organizations, or social conventions." "The Cynic battle," Foucault continues, "is an explicit, intentional, and constant aggression directed at humanity in general, at humanity in its real life"—with humanity understood here as a fabrication, as something that can be reworked.[15] Like every other philosophy of its time, Cynicism seeks to transform moral attitudes, passions, and appetites, but it does so by attacking the structures and conventions of which these attitudes are symptomatic. The Cynic seeks to release humanity from its current attachments, where Cynic interventions grow in strength and reach to the extent that they manage to cause outrage, bringing unthinking commitments to the surface, rendering them visible and open to adjustment. By comparison, the "true life" of the conventional philosopher carries to perfection the virtues and qualities that are only said to be weakly expressed in ordinary lives. This is their distinctly conservative, if not reactionary, assignment.

Change the Value of the Currency

The distinction between Diogenes and his opponents may be further drawn by exploring the significance of Diogenes's encounter with the Delphic Oracle, high priestess at the Temple of Apollo. Just as Socrates received the prophecy that he was the wisest man, Diogenes received his own divination—or at least, forged a "counterfeit oracle" of his own.[16] Diogenes's encounter has been described as "a rascal's take on the dignity of oracles,"[17] a parody of the Socratic legend.[18] Diogenes, so the story goes, was instructed to "change the value of the currency" or *parakharattein to nomisma*. The word *nomisma* has multiple

The Cynic seeks to release humanity from its current attachments, where Cynic interventions grow in strength and reach to the extent that they cause outrage, bringing unthinking commitments to the surface.

significations, referring to legal tender, but also norms, customs, and laws.[19] Insofar as the prophecy invites some kind of confrontation with or questioning of the *nomos* or law, this instruction to change the value of the currency might be interpreted as inciting subversive if not criminal activity. The phrase became a defining idea in the life of the Cynic, where the Delphic injunction is seen as recommending a stance the Cynic must take in relation to any social convention in circulation. The command to change the value of the currency is nonetheless ambiguous. In a limited and straightforward sense, a coin can be devalued by defacing it to such an extent that it may no longer be used in exchange for goods and services. According to tradition, Diogenes's father was in charge of the mint at Sinope. An unearthed collection of defaced coins testifies to the story that during this period someone was busy defacing counterfeit, "barbarian" coins with a large chisel stamp, to remove them from circulation and thereby maintain the value of the true, authentic currency.[20] This strict interpretation of the Delphic injunction is reflected in how the phrase is often translated, as "defacing the currency."[21] Against this more literal interpretation, Foucault favors the idea of altering rather than simply obliterating (false) value. Extending Foucault's analysis, it is indeed tempting to interpret the Cynic injunction, *parakharattein to nomisma*, as a pre-Nietzschean invitation to the "revaluation of all values."[22] To give a concrete example, the defacement or the removal of an effigy (such as the reigning monarch) could also be its replacement or adjustment so that the message changes from one of veneration to a depiction of exploitation and sanctioned brutality. Or, rather than simply reveal what some might see as the brutal truth of a money-based economy, the effigy could be replaced by a rival image, indicating that another way of organizing existence is possible. This would "enable the coin to circulate with its true value," so to speak, since it is now stamped "with another, better, and more adequate effigy."[23] Here, by producing a better currency, the Cynic endeavors to show that the conventional currency is the original counterfeit. To the extent that the idea of a currency represents social conventions more generally, by challenging it the Cynic demonstrates that our lives are, in a similar way, "no more than counterfeit."[24] It is in this sense that the injunction to change the value of the currency might be understood as an attempted revaluation of values: coins that once had value become worthless, and things once considered worthless gain value.

The life of the Cynic perhaps embodies this switch by putting its conception of "the true currency with its true value into circulation."[25] This life undermines existing systems of value; it seeks to break "totally and on every point with the traditional forms of existence."[26] As Foucault argues, by making a spectacle of itself in this way,

Cynicism asserts the need for "an *other* life ... a life whose otherness must lead to the change of the world. An *other* life for an *other* world."[27] Cynicism asserts that an entirely different order of existence is available to us (another currency could be minted), though not without struggle. By pursuing a mode of life that is radically opposed to its surroundings, Cynicism exposes those surroundings in all their constraint. Unlike the Platonic conception of another transcendent world (the realm of the Forms), which is used to denigrate this world in favor of one higher but forever withheld; the Cynic conception of an *other* life is developed through an immanent critique of this life, pushing it to explode its confines.

On Sophistication

Despite all these points of distinction, it is still tempting to interpret Diogenes and the Cynic way of life he is associated with as if they advocate a return to the animalistic. This raises once more the suspicion that Cynics were just anticulture and anticivilization, with little to offer but a celebration of base impulses. The Cynic injunction to live in accord with nature might hereby be interpreted as an invitation to indulge natural desires and inclinations often at other people's expense. But Cynic philosophy taught the opposite, demonstrating through deliberate self-impoverishment how very little a resourceful practitioner needs to survive. Cynic philosophy did not give free reign to every appetite, but explored how the appetite is a product of habit and artificial conditioning. As such, it can be retrained. It is possible to develop new and perhaps better appetites.

A suspicion nonetheless remains that the Cynics were so preoccupied by the call of nature that they were somehow blind to the technological and cultural achievements of humankind. But this would be a caricature. Cynics were not idealistic enough to pit nature against culture or civilization, at least not as concepts or as an intellectual exercise, though they were perfectly adept at pitting "nature" against "culture" in practice—the Cynic who would pass wind instead of pleasantries, for instance; Cynics were notorious for consuming vast quantities of beans for the accompanying effects. In relation to matters of culture and civilization, Cynic objections were focused and situated, confronting, as Sloterdijk argues, "what civilization offers by way of comfortable seductions to entice people to serve its ends," namely, a whole set of "ideals, ideas about duty, promises of redemption, hopes of immortality, goals for ambition, positions of power, careers, arts, riches."[28] Though each notion operates differently and requires its own individual riposte, what these seductions share is their dependence on a metaphor of elevation. Here the Cynic's depraved, bestial behavior can be viewed as a pointed tactic, used to disrupt cultural conventions by associating them with their apparent opposite.

By resorting to animality, and by giving bestial acts a certain priority over more refined "human" traits, the Cynic was not an environmental activist in nascent form arguing for the higher nobility of nature. A normative conception of nature does not appear to provide a foundation for Cynic philosophy. Interpretations vary, of course, but those commentators who are suspicious of the common view that nature was Cynicism's foundational attachment claim that, on a closer look at the anecdotes collected by Laertius that "purport to quote Diogenes [of Sinope] verbatim, nowhere does he show any interest in nature as a philosophical concept."[29] If Diogenes should be admitted to the "Ancestral Gallery of Ecological Consciousness," as Sloterdijk puts it, it is only because he managed to transform the theme of refuse (namely, his own shit) into a dominant preoccupation.[30] The production of waste material is recognized as an important feature of human existence.

There is something undeniably rude about Cynic behavior, in both senses of the word. Not only is Cynicism ill mannered, it appears to lack sophistication. For some, Diogenes's attacks on social convention may give the impression of being as simplistic and poorly thought through as they are offensive. Once more, however, it is worth wondering where our taste for sophistication and this tendency to criticize Cynicism for its lack of refinement originate. Borrowing perhaps from the philosophical idea of wisdom, sophistication is again associated with a metaphor of elevation, where the wise rise above the workaday diversions of the majority in their refinement. So utterly dominant is this metaphor of elevation that its attackers can be understood only through its lens. They are either dismissed as ignorant of higher things, or celebrated for their own embedded, submerged, perhaps even disavowed sophistication. The latter argument achieves an evaluative reversal that is patently absurd, though it somehow makes sense to the cultured. There is perhaps no better example of this than the perverse justification of Samuel Beckett's Nobel Prize awarded in 1969 for writing that "*acquires its elevation*" from "*the destitution of modern man*." Accordingly, the extreme degradation and reduction of life to its base materials found in Beckett's work can only be perceived (by the defender of humanistic culture) as a negative image of all that elevates humanity above the muck that Beckett depicts.[31] "Look how sophisticated we are, we even notice the dirt."

On Shitting

Diogenes was not lacking in the arts of sophistication. He had mastered that ancient display of urbanity known as oration, if only to subvert it. It is claimed that after one particularly well-received public oration, at which "a large audience listened to this speech of Diogenes with great appreciation," Diogenes "stopped speaking, squatted, and performed an unseemly act "[32] Unsurprisingly, this caused great insult. One interpretation of what Diogenes was up to here is that he was authenticating his Cynicism by squatting before an audience. Surely, having debased himself in this way, Diogenes had nothing more to gain from abiding by the falseness of public theater and conventional rhetoric: "Because he has nothing to lose, he can tell the truth and, therefore, may be worth listening to."[33] This moment—something his audience failed to understand—was the point after which they should *begin* listening, rather than turn away. Having disgraced himself so completely, Diogenes had no reason to flatter or dupe them. His authority as Cynic philosopher relied upon the assurance this act gave his audience that Diogenes was not bound by any convention, including those rules that govern social intercourse.

The significance of this scatological episode is testified by the extent to which it has become one of the signature acts of Diogenes's philosophy. But there is a danger in giving it priority. There is a risk of reducing Cynicism to this single act, as if the key maneuver in any Cynic engagement is to first authenticate one's Cynicism by fidelity, by an act of shameless courage that places the Cynic center-ground and beyond doubt. Working against this reductive tendency, there is another approach to understanding Cynicism, one that views it as a more tactical engagement, once more involving the kind of situated flexibility and inventiveness one might expect of a militant, nondogmatic philosopher. This engagement begins with the context it seeks to subvert and defines itself in tactical opposition to that context, paying far less attention to matters of fealty to Cynic tradition (which risk essentializing Cynicism and turning its gaze inward). A slightly different interpretation, then, one that does not simply understand squatting before an audience as a gesture of self-authentication, is to point out that Diogenes not only excreted in public, he did so precisely when his audience was most enraptured. The deliberate timing of the act is key. Diogenes was not claiming to exist entirely outside the norms that governed social life, since he had already shown how well he could abide by them (up until that point his audience had been enraptured). He was not ignorant of finer things, perhaps overcome by base impulses and unable to act otherwise. The problem that Diogenes presents is the fact he chooses to act in such a way, and does so *from a position of sophistication*, namely, from a position that had, up until that point, abided by shared norms of public conduct. One way of interpreting this scatological act, then, is to understand it as an attack on cultured refinement, a blast from below, by someone who is all too familiar with what he attacks.

Diogenes not only
excreted in public,
he did so precisely
when his audience
was most enraptured.

Another way of approaching the problem of Diogenes's base behavior (which included public masturbation) is to observe that if he had wished above all else to pursue the animal life, there is no reason why he should have chosen to do so in Athens. If his was a simple regression to the animalistic, it might have been pursued anywhere. What remains significant about Diogenes's example is that he remained in Athens, and not in any back alley, but prominently displayed in the *agora*. Diogenes situates himself in society as an agent of cultural transformation. Confronting the problem with characteristic candor, Sloterdijk argues: "Diogenes taught masturbation by practical example, as cultural progress, mind you, not as regression to the animalistic."[34] Here Sloterdijk comes close to the position Emperor Julian occupies (see chapter 4), by claiming that the shameless behavior of the Cynic seeks to demonstrate "that people as a rule are ashamed for the wrong reasons [for their bodily emissions, for example] ... while they remain unmoved by their irrational and ugly practices, their greed, unfairness, cruelty, vanity, prejudice, and blindness."[35] But Sloterdijk goes much further than Julian (as one would expect), arguing that for the Cynic, the very finest customs we live by, "including those dealing with shame," are "perverted." For this reason, the Cynic refuses to be "led by the nose by deeply engrained commandments regarding shame." Building on such deep-set suspicion, shameless behavior sets out to test all social conformisms that uphold the operations of empire. Against the conceit of such unthinking conformism, "Diogenes turns the tables. He literally shits on the perverted norms," to quote Sloterdijk again. Diogenes "set himself in opposition to the political training in virtue of all systems," where these systems depend on shame to secure their purchase.[36]

As Foucault argues along somewhat similar lines, if the soul is to be educated, it must be convinced that somewhere, somehow its activities and inclinations are visible. Ancient philosophy inaugurated a cultural/educational trajectory that would make the self, the individual, individuated subject appear transparent to its own introverted interrogations, sometimes adding an external agent (an idea that was clearly taken up by Christianity), where for a Stoic philosopher such as Epictetus, God dwells within us. Consequently, all impure thoughts and dirty actions sully that divine presence as much as they do the Stoic practitioner.[37] One must live in private as if nothing remains concealed, developing the necessary inhibitions and restraints. To challenge this framework of subjugation, the Cynic opts to radicalize the idea that nothing is concealed, by acting it out. The Cynic responds to the injunction that the true life is the life that has nothing to hide, by hiding nothing. The Cynic does everything in the open, having given up the security of a home or retreat to privacy. This removes or at least places in question the constraining influence of a conscience that is designed precisely for those private spaces that must be convinced of their culpability. Since these private spaces have become the residence of the conscience, this "staging of life [by the Cynic] in its material and everyday reality under the real gaze of others, of everyone else, or at any rate of the greatest possible number of others,"[38] can be understood as an attempt to render the moral order imposed by the conscience inoperable, or at least open to question.

Shame, Humiliation, Laughter

In placing shame and humiliation at the center of its educational practice, Cynicism brings to expression the tendency of all educational relations to shame and humiliate those who are to be educated. Here, as with aggression, the ancient Cynics acted out and thereby drew attention to the inherent humiliations of educational experience, finding radical potential in accentuating what some might prefer to deny. Diogenes actively ridiculed those who would have him be their teacher. According to one account, when someone expressed a wish to study philosophy with Diogenes, he "gave him a fish to carry and told him to follow in his footsteps." Ashamed, and perhaps a little perplexed, the man threw it away: "When Diogenes came across him some time later, Diogenes burst out laughing and said, 'Our friendship was brought to an end by a fish!'"[39]

Cynicism brings to expression the tendency of all educational relations to shame and humiliate those who are to be educated.

It seems what the would-be disciple failed to understand is that to practice Cynicism one undergoes repeated humiliation; to carry the fish (or cheese in a different version of the story) would be to act as if one were Diogenes's slave—an unbearable humiliation in Athenian society. As Sloterdijk argues, the Cynic has a taste for humiliation, understanding that shame is "the most intimate social fetter, which binds us, *before* all concrete rules of conscience, to universal standards of behaviour."[40] As a "main factor in social conformisms," shame operates as "the switch point where external controls are transformed into internal controls."[41] For that reason, shame and humiliation are at the center of a Cynic revolt.

The Cynic was not alone in the deliberate use of humiliation as a spiritual exercise. As Foucault argues, we can see traces of this "Cynic game of humiliation" in Christian humility: "From Cynic humiliation to Christian humility there is," he claims, "an entire history of the humble, of disgrace, shame, and scandal through shame, which is very important historically and, once again, quite foreign to the standard morality of the Greeks and Romans."[42] Foucault argues that it is nevertheless important to "distinguish the future Christian humility, which is a state, a mental attitude manifesting itself and testing itself in the humiliations one suffers," from Cynic humiliation. The latter can be understood as a game with conventions of honor and dishonor in which the Cynic attempts to escape the order of shame and submission that disgrace enforces. Another way of putting this is to say that the Cynic asserts his or her sovereignty and perverse mastery *through* these tests of humiliation, "whereas Christian humiliation, or rather, humility, is a renunciation of oneself."[43] According to Foucault's rendering of what he calls Christian techniques of the self, "the more we discover the truth of ourselves, the more we must renounce ourselves."[44] The Christian self that is the object of so much introspection never appears in its final, satisfactory form, which is not to say that it is an illusion. Rather, the Christian self is "much too real."[45] It is filled with temptations, appetites, and seductions that have to be driven out, or brought to harness, as part of the (by design, unrealizable) Christian duty to discover what one is.

Again, despite these points of distinction, it is still difficult to imagine how the Cynic pursuit of penury and humiliation did not, after all, share much in attitude and experience with the Christian ascetic and monk. To counter the overall impression that Cynics were in a state of pious self-denial, it is worth drawing attention to the role of farce and comedy in Cynic philosophy. Like Cynic shamelessness, Cynic humor was designed to outrage its victims, since outrage expresses the very conventions the Cynic seeks to upset. But Cynic humor was potentially disarming, too. As Bakhtin argues (in relation to Menippean satire, a Cynic literary genre), laughter can serve to demolish distance and undermine hierarchy: "Laughter has the remarkable power of making an object come up close, of drawing it into a zone of crude contact where one can finger it familiarly on all sides, turn it upside down, inside out, peer at it from above and below, break open its external shell, look into its center, doubt it, take it apart, dismember it, lay it bare and expose it."[46] Bakhtin is perhaps a little optimistic about the revolutionary potential of laughter, though in Cynic hands and combined with the techniques outlined above, its subversive force can well be imagined. Bakhtin associates this kind of laugher with "fearlessness," claiming that laughter "demolishes fear and piety before an object" by bringing it close, or down to earth, so to speak.[47] Hence Cynic comedy, as it is pictured here, does not simply bring hidden prejudices and commitments to expression, with these appearing as a direct result of its provocations. It brings them home because only in the form it reduces them to—the less venerable form of the butt of a joke—will such objects shed their respectable clothing and submit to investigation. This connection with fearlessness is important, as it emphasizes that Cynic laughter was not based in a cozy, comfortable comedy, but was on the verge of becoming decidedly unfunny. Through comedy, the Cynic pushes sardonic mirth "to the point that it becomes intolerable insolence."[48] Cynic wit always carried with it an element of danger. Techniques varied by context. Parody, for example, was used by Diogenes to mock the authority of reason. Accordingly, Diogenes mimicked the conventional philosophical form of a syllogism to justify theft, where the "butt of the joke is its form"—a "jarring contrast between the formal protocols of reason and the paradoxically Cynic" conclusion it leads to.[49] Crucially, Cynic humor involves the audience it berates, since it does not explain itself and requires the audience to fill in the gaps; the audience must supply an understanding of the norms that are being subverted in order to get the joke.

Unruly Disciples

The educational reach of Cynicism clearly exceeds the laughter as well as the deliberate aggressions and humiliations inflicted by Diogenes on his contemporaries. When Cynic philosophy was not directly exemplified through the life of a Cynic practitioner, it was conveyed through brief anecdotes, recollected gestures and retorts, ironic encounters, and witty remarks. Open to alteration, these quips were designed to be "as portable and memorable as jokes."[50] This accounts for the endurance of Cynicism in the absence of Cynic theory, by contrast to other philosophical schools that bequeathed relatively stable doctrines or teachings. Cynic sayings were passed on by means sharply contrasted to those of the dogmatic philosophical schools, whose transmission consisted, to quote

Foucault, in "reactualizing a forgotten and misunderstood core of thought in order to make it the point of departure and source of authority."[51] It was not a matter of defining oneself in relation to what a figure such as Aristotle or Plato had originally said, for instance.[52] Cynics had a very different relationship to their predecessors. Episodes from the lives of past Cynics were recalled not because these episodes and their doctrinal content had been forgotten (it mattered little if the episodes recounted were actual occurrences or mythical constructs). Rather, they were recalled because today's philosopher might no longer be "equal to these examples" owing to some sort of decline, enfeeblement, or decadence that had diluted our capacity for Cynicism.[53] Past Cynics were remembered to provoke present actors to reconsider their conduct, and perhaps to enable "the strength of conduct" exemplified in the actions of past Cynics "to be restored" to those lacking courage.[54] As explored in the next chapter, attempts to live up to Cynic philosophy were many and various, and always only partial.

FEAR THE MOB: ANTIQUE AND MEDIEVAL IDEALIZATIONS

Diogenes accumulated disciples by accident and retained them only as long as they would not be shaken off. This foregrounded a very different understanding of the relationship between (a normally revered) philosopher-teacher and (a closely associated) disciple. It testified to the presence of humiliation, rejection, and aggression at the center of the teaching relation. This reflected the treatment Diogenes apparently received at the hands of Antisthenes, pupil of Socrates and proto-Cynic, who was notoriously hostile to would-be pupils and beat Diogenes with his staff for coming too close.[1] There were variations on the theme; Crates (who was Diogenes pupil) famously converted Metrocles to Cynicism with a well-timed and kindly fart.[2] Laertius gives the names of about half a dozen members of Diogenes's little clan of associates, some by their nicknames,[3] suggesting they were well-known eccentrics.[4] In addition to Crates, who is by far the most famous, Monimus of Syracuse is worth mention since he appears to further extend Diogenes' hostility to the pretensions of philosophy.[5] It is claimed that Monimus never spoke a word "to match the saying 'know thyself,' nor such familiar watchwords" from the Greek philosophical tradition. "No, the squalid mendicant surpassed them all, for he declared all human supposition to be illusion."[6] Apparently, Monimus was suspicious of education in all its forms, declaring that "it was better to lack sight than education. For under one affliction you fall to the ground, in the other deep underground."[7]

Hostile to conventional understandings of education, dismissive of hangers-on, Cynic teaching was not modeled on the life of study, but on the life of provocations and bowel movements. If it had a philosophy of education, this philosophy was improvised and scatological, designed to transgress our basic assumptions of what education should look and feel like. Given its attachment to the brief earthly existence of each scurrilous Cynic, rather than to a doctrine or text that ensures continuity across generations, the descent of Cynicism is erratic and episodic. The history of Cynicism is complicated too by the fact that the name is itself unreliable; to assemble a history around this term, to collect together all historical fragments and references to the words Cynic/Cynical/Cynicism, is to restrict that history to a word that has already been much abused

Cynic teaching was
not modeled on the life
of study, but on the
life of provocations
and bowel movements.

and distorted. It might be better, indeed, to assemble a history of Cynicism around a broader set of militant themes. This would be a history of "forms, modes, and styles of life" rather than a history of philosophy in the more typical sense.[8] It might contain little or no reference at all to the word Cynicism. But such a history remains to be told. Although this book stays fixated on the term, on its gradual adjustment—and is for that reason limited by its concern with everything that has adopted the name "Cynic"—the point of focus is to explore just exactly why that term was produced in such a way as to remain intrinsically unreliable and evasive.

The Idealized Cynic

It has been argued that the history of Cynicism is one in which an opposition is repeatedly played out between true (ancient) and false (modern), or venerable and base C/cynicisms.[9] Venerable Cynicisms have origins that always remain just out of reach. They are beyond reach in the sense that they are accessible only secondhand, but also in the sense that Diogenes—the prototypical reference point—was not the first Cynic. Even in antiquity, commentators suspected that Cynicism antedated Antisthenes (Diogenes's reputed teacher), and could be extended back to the time before Heracles, son of Zeus. This linkage back to the Greek pantheon, to deities rather than historical figures, might sound like a step too far. But this connection could be instructive if those deities are understood to reflect early Greek sensibility for a form of wisdom, a "cunning intelligence," that fourth-century Greek philosophy subsequently turned its back on and lost.[10] Perhaps only Cynic philosophy carried forward the canny wisdom of the gods, maintaining in its improvised Cynic lifestyle some appreciation of the situated craftiness of those deities who operated within a world that was not yet fully formed, who lived in a context where objects and relations between objects had yet to stabilize. The gods, like the Cynics, lived by their wits.

Cynicism can also be traced back to earlier forms in Greek ethnography. Sixth- and fifth-century Greek ethnographers recounted tales of idealized barbarian races—noble, one-eyed-griffin-plagued peoples and justice-loving, long-lived dog-headed creatures. They used the outsider perspectives these races offered as a ploy or device to safely reflect on more "civilized" cultures.[11] When dealing with Diogenes—in many respects also considered to be a "barbarian" character from the edges of the Greek world—many commentators would idealize him in a similar way. They would make use of Diogenes as a foreign character who could be put to work offering an external point of view. Within such accounts it was necessary to "purge his portrait of any features that might shock or keep off potential followers."[12] In that form Diogenes could be safely deployed as a cultural critic. It was necessary, in other words, for the first authors who described Cynic practices, and who gave an account of its key players, to debunk certain aspects of Cynic tradition, and find its hidden qualities elsewhere. Curiously, the descent of Cynicism, its retention, depended on efforts to "expel the Cynic and his mode of existence from the honourable and recognized philosophical field." This act of expulsion recuperated Cynic philosophy by referring it to a "universally valid Cynicism," which might be integrated with other philosophies and points of view.[13] By appeal to an idealized Cynicism that sidestepped the most uncomfortable teachings of Diogenes and his life in the barrel, the educated and cultured would claim Cynicism for their own, setting in train a series of maneuvers that would transform Cynic philosophy almost beyond recognition.

An early example of Cynic co-option can be found in Stoic philosophy. Stoic philosophers were determined to connect their third-century BCE founder, Zeno of Citium, to Socrates. This resulted in the proposed succession, which ran Socrates–Antisthenes–Diogenes–Crates–Zeno, where Diogenes serves as a crucial link that authenticates the tradition of Stoic philosophy, affirming its Socratic pedigree.[14] Echoes of this Stoic co-option can still be found in contemporary scholarship, which reads Cynicism through the self-sufficient, pleasure-regulating, ethical principles of Stoic philosophy. The decline of Cynicism can, apparently, be understood through a similar lens, as the necessary replacement of a laudable but basic Cynic philosophy with a more sophisticated Stoic alternative. Hence the claim that the Cynics were "raising serious problems" even if they gave "unsatisfactory answers"—leaving it to the Stoics to take forward their investigations.[15] Or the following argument: "With the flowering of Stoicism and Epicureanism in the next generation, Cynicism ceased to offer an ethical option powerful enough to withstand the more complex attractions of these rival philosophers, who reinterpreted and incorporated its most effective contributions to ethics." This leads to the subsequent claim that it was only once Cynicism had been "ousted from the mainstream of Hellenistic philosophy" that it "degenerated into popular moralizing, satirical commonplaces, and charlatan street preaching."[16] Here, then, we encounter an evaluative framework in which Cynicism just about retains its dignity so long as it maintains association with the mainstream of Hellenistic philosophy. Only once that connection was lost did it degenerate into the form of a popular, street philosophy.

This judgmental frame is remarkably enduring. To gather up a few other examples; in his influential 1937 study, Dudley argued that the "persuasive charm" of a figure such as Diogenes could not last: The "weakness of Cynicism" lay in its "inability" (reluctance?) to "give an account of itself." Though Diogenes was an inspirational character, as his direct influence waned subsequent Cynicisms degenerated. Unable to "appeal to the intelligence"[17] they became confined to the life of the street in all its unreflective stupidity. A decade later in his *History of Western Philosophy* Bertrand Russell declared: "What was best in the Cynic doctrine passed over into Stoicism, which was an altogether more complete and rounded philosophy."[18] More recently, the entry in the *Oxford Companion to Philosophy* concludes: "many a Cynic ... was doubtless no more than a tramp," and presumably, as such, had nothing to contribute to philosophy.[19]

Arguments such as these are troubling. They seem uncomfortably close to those that once sought to dismiss or sanitize Cynicism when Cynic "tramps" were a force to be reckoned with. Cynicism survived well into the Roman Empire as a popular philosophy, a scurrilous way of life for the "disenfranchised and discontented."[20] Given that reports of its existence were themselves designed to co-opt Cynicism and place it in the service of the well-to-do, it is hard to judge whether or not it had indeed degenerated, or simply been developed or adjusted to new circumstances. What we can be sure of, however, is that this street Cynicism was an adapted form of that philosophy, resulting from the process of selective mimesis (rather than institutional descent) that had passed Cynicism down through the centuries. We cannot accurately assess the vitality of Cynic philosophy in its street-level form, because most of the sketches and sayings on which we depend were composed and passed on by commentators who were not themselves Cynics, and had at best only partial affinity for what Cynic philosophy was attempting to achieve. It does appear that within the alienating, "colossal bureaucratic apparatus" of the Roman Empire—"whose inner and outer workings an individual could not fathom or influence"—Cynic (as well as Christian) sects found a secure footing in popular discontent.[21] As Sloterdijk observes, moralistic, popular resistance "against the social and human circumstances of the empire had swelled into a powerful spiritual current."[22] Half a millennium since Diogenes, the "dogs" were howling in large packs. Given its appeal among the lower orders, Cynicism of this base type had to be categorically rejected by more cultured commentators if anything was to be rescued for respectable philosophy. Consequently, it can be encountered only in a distorted form, described by those who found street Cynicism decidedly abhorrent. The examples of Epictetus, Lucian, and Julian will be considered below.

Epictetus

The Stoic philosopher Epictetus—a freed slave whose life spanned the first and second centuries, and who was a proponent, after Socrates, of the idea that one's philosophy must be lived[23]—was careful to distinguish his own nostalgic conception of Cynicism from what he called the "sad spectacle of today's Cynics,"[24] who, as one scholar characterizes his point of view, "mimicked their masters in nothing other than cutting farts."[25] By adopting Diogenes as a Stoic icon, Epictetus transformed key markers of Cynic philosophy. He treated Diogenes as an exemplar of philosophical self-mastery and control, a philosopher who should be admired because he was protected by nothing but his honor: "Honour is his house, his gate, his guards, his cloak of darkness."[26] Though Epictetus sometimes made use of the "vivid, brusque, anecdotal style" that characterized Cynic teaching, he also made use of rigorous, systematic argument.[27] And even if Epictetus shared with Cynicism a disdain for mere learning or eloquence, and a penchant for what have been described as "shocking illustrations—chamber pots, greasy fingers, wobbly legs, dunghills, cracked saucepans, and the like,"[28] his appeal to Cynicism was nonetheless highly idealized. Epictetus's objections to other, lowlier conceptions of Cynicism might nonetheless be contextualized, given that he needed to secure an income from his teaching, and had a reputation to uphold.[29] In his attempt to reclaim a more respectable Cynicism, Epictetus recalls the image of the beggar Cynic who "hectors everyone who crosses his path," and declares: "if that's how you picture Cynicism, it's better you keep your distance."[30] The proper response to such cheap imitators is to give them a wide berth. Attempting to counter the idea that Cynics should live on the street in a state of squalor, Epictetus explains that the Cynic "shouldn't be so filthy that he drives people away"; rather, "his ruggedness should be of a clean and healthy kind."[31] From this perspective, the Cynic's body should be "an advertisement of the merits of his simple open-air life,"[32] a spectacle of health, beauty, and masculine accomplishment (rather than a site of struggle on which the imprints of adversity are wrought). Female Cynics were not unheard of, but Epictetus has only men in mind. His vision of the Cynic is a man of honor with a mind "purer than the sun."[33]

Against this particular idealization—and at the risk of drawing my treatment of Epictetus to a premature halt—it is worth turning our attention to the case of Hipparchia, who married the Cynic Crates (Diogenes's pupil). As the most famous female Cynic from Greek antiquity, Hipparchia was treated by later commentators as an exception, with most women presumably not up to the calling of philosophy, and certainly not up to the challenge of a lived philosophy such as Cynicism. Perhaps Crates managed well enough despite the presence of Hipparchia, Epictetus suggests, but all other women would be a distraction. If the Cynic marries, Epictetus advises, "he must get a kettle to heat water for the baby … wool for his wife … oil, a cot, a cup, and many pieces of crockery." And with so much drudgery and distraction of that sort: "What then will become of the King, whose duty it is to be overseer over the rest of mankind."[34] Unfortunate associations between Cynicism and women were clearly being marginalized and explained away here.

With the inclusion of Hipparchia in Cynic folklore, it seems that the challenge posed by ancient Cynicism to social convention included those rites that governed the role of women in society. Hipparchia has been described for that reason as the "first feminist."[35] It is claimed by extension that ancient Cynicism was "basically non-sexist."[36] This is debatable. Cynicism (or at least Crates) may have embraced Hipparchia and thereby undermined social constraints that debarred women from engaging in parrhesia, for instance (recall that only free-born, propertied men were free to speak in this way and address the Greek *polis*). This inclusive gesture may well have reflected a Cynic point of view that there is no difference between men and women when it comes to their aptitude for philosophy, even for a philosophy as demanding as Cynicism. But it remains the case that Hipparchia derives her fame from marriage to Crates[37] (despite his best attempts to put her off,[38] it has to be said, which might be interpreted as testimony to her fortitude and commitment). Hipparchia's induction to (male-dominated) philosophy can itself be viewed as a mixed blessing.[39] It is true that Antisthenes apparently declared "virtue is the same for women as for men"[40] and "we ought to make love to such women as will feel a proper gratitude,"[41] while Diogenes "advocated a community of wives, recognizing no other marriage than a union of the man who persuades with the woman who consents."[42] Recognizing that women should be able to express some kind of preference in sexual relations, and that they might even approach the "virtuous" achievements of men, might have scandalized the patriarchy of ancient Greece, but it hardly places women on equal footing. Nonetheless, the place of women, or at least Hipparchia, within Cynic philosophy was sufficiently awkward to provoke later writers such as Epictetus to diminish their significance. This would eventually lead to a situation where Cynic "openness to women and other outsiders was effectively reversed." This reversal was complete once "Diogenes' apothegms, either chosen or invented for their misogynist or racist humor, were incorporated into the lower-level grammar curriculum in antiquity" to train boys in the Greek language.[43]

Lucian

In the second century, Lucian—an extraordinary rhetorician who issued from the eastern outskirts of the Roman Empire—transformed Cynic contempt into a satirical art form, influencing writers as diverse and distantly related as Desiderius Erasmus, Thomas More, François Rabelais, Jonathan Swift, Henry Fielding, and Denis Diderot. Lucian's merciless account of the self-immolation of a contemporary Cynic sect leader, in *The Death of Peregrinus*, again helped distinguish the cultivated man with a taste for highbrow Cynicism from the street Cynics below.[44] His comic dialogue, *The Runaways*, continued with an attack on sham philosophers: "Every city is filled with such upstarts, particularly with those who enter the names of Diogenes, Antisthenes, and Crates as their patrons and enlist in the army of the dog."[45] Their offense, quite simply, was to have brought philosophy into disrepute, tarnishing its reputation before the "unschooled" who would mistake sham philosophy for the thing itself.[46] Against these sham Cynics, Lucian's encomium to his apparent teacher, the Cynic Demonax, helped set up a respectable, highly idealized alternative.[47]

Lucian's complaint against sham Cynicism was also directed at education more generally. His ire was of a sort that bemoans the current state of education for the love of what it might otherwise be, for the freedom and elevation it promises but fails to deliver. The debased reality of being a household tutor—which was a dominant educational model of the time—was, Lucian decided, surely too much for anyone to bear who is "even to the slightest degree cultured."[48] Lucian's *On Salaried Posts in Great Houses* is an attempt to dissuade Greek philosophers from taking up such servile, deeply claustrophobic, and compromised positions, where the educator is trapped within a dysfunctional, manipulative context, a situation in which the resident employee is revered and demeaned in the same gesture. In this account, Lucian seems moved by the plight of the household educator out of respect for philosophy and its vision of a higher form of education. Even though Lucian is notorious for his mocking tone and tactical evasiveness, there is no Cynic contempt for the high ideals of education here.

In Lucian's work, ancient Cynics are once more offered as the model against which the debasement of contemporary Cynicism (and philosophy) is to be measured. But Lucian is also careful in places to stress the "unbridgeable historical distance between his own era and that of Diogenes." This implies, so it has been argued, "the impossibility, or even absurdity, of practical imitation of the Cynic lifestyle," and justifies Lucian's own turn instead "toward a *literary* recreation of the Cynic."[49] Of the many characters who make an appearance in Lucian's satires, it has been claimed that Menippus (an ancient Cynic from the third century BCE) offers "the most succinct embodiment" of Lucian's position.[50] As a fictional persona, Menippus allows Lucian to challenge tradition and express through him a kind of Cynic derision at the "pretense to knowledge on the part of professional thinkers."[51] But Lucian's Cynicism is nonetheless enclosed within the limits of its satirical form. His Cynicism can be understood as the "controlled evocation of a role," where Lucian avoids identifying too completely with the part. The audience encounters a carefully staged Cynicism in his work, a Cynicism confined to its dramatic, fictional context. His relation to Cynicism is one of admiring but ironic detachment.[52]

In Sloterdijk's analysis, the seriocomic Cynical impulse is now split between the educated satirist who inherits the Cynic's sardonic wit, and a low-level sect led by figures such as Peregrinus, composed of "the unstable and resentful, bums and moral zealots, outsiders and narcissists" that have become all too earnest and serious in their devotions.[53] As Foucault characterizes him, Peregrinus was an "ostentatious vagabond … no doubt linked to the anti-Roman popular movements of Alexandria, addressing his teaching at Rome to the *idiotai* (those without culture or social and political status)."[54] Lucian lampoons Peregrinus for the manner of his death, claiming to have witnessed his self-immolation upon a pyre at the Olympic Games in 165 CE. This vain act just about sums up everything that is wrong with street Cynicism in Lucian's view, with its "tendency [as Sloterdijk interprets] to supercilious, naïve, pompous, gushing fanaticism, in which vanity and masochistic martyrlike characteristics" are combined. But if the street Cynics were "the moral despisers of their epoch," Lucian is hardly any better in Sloterdijk's view. Lucian appears as "the despiser of the despisers, the moralist of the moralisers." His "satire is a cultivated attack on the uncultivated beggar-moralists and wailers, that is, a kind of master's satire on the intellectual simpletons of his time." In *The Death of Peregrinus* the victims of Cynic comedy are no longer "representatives of vain knowledge" and cultural conceit, but the downtrodden and dispossessed.[55] Lucian's Cynicism "denounces the critics of power to the powerful and cultivated as ambitious lunatics." Effectively, Cynic critique has changed sides, its point of view "trimmed to the irony of those in power."[56] With Lucian, Cynic humor became "a function of literature," and this for Sloterdijk was very much to its detriment.[57]

Julian

In the fourth century, Julian—a Roman notable, administrator, and philosopher who eventually became emperor from 361 to 363 CE—devoted some time to the study of Cynicism, goaded by the influence street Cynics were having on his soldiers and lower levels of the citizenry. He set out to challenge these bawdy imitators, who were, as he put it, "moving from city to city or camp to camp and insulting the rich and prominent in all such places while associating with society's dregs."[58] In this apparently debased, descendant form, Cynicism was clearly still a going concern.

By the example of their disruptive existence, street Cynics offered their own interpretation of the Cynic legacy. Julian, like those before him, found himself confronted by an enduring, lived philosophy that addressed a wider and, in his eyes, "not very cultured public," as Foucault puts it, drawing its recruits "from outside the educated elites that usually practiced philosophy."[59] These false Cynics are once again portrayed as outright charlatans, pretending to cultivate wisdom, but succeeding only in the cultivation of their ignorance. Particularly incensed by his contemporary, the Cynic Heracleios, Julian denounced in him "a savage attitude of mind that knows nothing of what is good, fair and decent."[60] Devoid of respect, operating without reverence for the Gods, hell-bent on destroying all beauty, honesty, and goodness, trampling justice and honor under foot, and perhaps worst of all, turning philosophy into a laughing stock,[61] street Cynics were promoting a "barbarian" creed, and were doing so right at the center of the Roman Empire. These Cynic pretenders should not be driven from the city, Julian decided. "Death by stoning would be more appropriate."[62] That might sound extreme, but there was precedent for this kind of violence, with a whole sequence of obstinate philosophers including Cynics exiled, flogged, or executed under the emperors Nero, Vespasian, and Domitian in the first century—a time, soon to pass, when even respectable philosophy posed a threat to imperial power.[63]

Julian's contrasting vision of a respectable Cynicism—a philosophy one might emulate in one's bearing, could practice at home, and celebrate in public—bore only a distant relation to its debased opposite. A Cynic of this variety would still speak the truth, fearlessly at times, yet without the insults and aggressions of the Cynic diatribe.

When delivered by the man of *paideia* (a man who obeyed the conventions and practices that governed and maintained the decorum of the Roman nobility[64]), such insights would be carefully expressed and could expect to be well received. To compound things further, Julian situates his Cynic within a philosophy of bodily denial, claiming that each body bears a certain "potentiality," insofar as it contains a soul that may achieve knowledge of higher things.[65] For Julian, the human soul occupies an intermediate position between the mortal and the divine. It must overcome that part of itself which is "changeful and multiform, something composite of anger and appetite, a many-headed monster." This part must be tamed, and "persuaded to obey the god within us," the "divine part" of the soul.[66] Since it contains immortal traces within itself, with the benefit of philosophy and due training, the human soul may approach the gods through subdued passions and increased self-knowledge. A divinely inspired education in philosophy releases the soul from its body, forming a person endowed with true understanding. There are many routes to divine knowledge, Julian concedes, but his own recuperated Cynicism ranks among the noblest.

Those who find themselves still tied to the body—and here we must insert the street Cynics Julian deplores—are by this definition alone, uneducated. The body distracts them, and ensures they remain "subject to false opinion instead of truth."[67] "Rapacious and depraved and no better than any one of the brute beasts,"[68] these inner-city out-casts have, by this account, entirely misunderstood the purpose of Cynic philosophy. As Julian declared in his lengthy oration "To the Uneducated Cynics,"[69] those who wish to become educated must look down on the body as a "jailer of the soul,"[70] a jailer to be escaped through rigorous training. This, Julian assures, is a task for which the true Cynic, the Cynic of his conception, is destined. Although this Cynic may be a harsh teacher at times (the noble Cynic demonstrates bodily discipline and speaks the "unembel-lished truth" without apparent regard for the sensibilities of his audience),[71] there were Cynics who also charmed their audiences into submission, and here Julian gives the example of Crates, softening once more the depiction of the Cynic as shameless and confrontational.[72] And on the delicate matter of Diogenes obeying "the call of nature" and emitting "unseemly noises" in public, surely, Julian won-ders, this rather odd practice was only designed to draw a contrast between these natural acts, and all the unnatural "rascally business"—"robbery of money, false accusations, unjust indictments"—that were, for Diogenes, "far more sordid and insupportable than his own" emissions.[73]

Julian recognizes that the path adopted by the noble Cynic is a difficult one, and that there are easier routes to wisdom. In defense of myth (which the Cynic has no time for), Julian argues that the original creators of myth were "like nannies who hang leather dolls above the cribs of teething infants, to distract them and alleviate their pain." This was the manner in which "those first mythologists supplied a steady stream of stories and legends to the fledgling souls of young men learning to fly and eager to be taught but not yet ready to absorb the undiluted truth."[74] A little falseness was necessary, Julian admits, to mitigate the pain and irritation that education must produce, as it reorients us to the truth. For more advanced study, myths can also help demonstrate that the truth of the world often lies concealed, hidden within riddles, and can be accessed only through the mediating influence of philosophy.[75] Finally, myths have served to protect the philosopher who acts as a personal physician[76] from the kind of retribution that blunt advice, that is to say advice not dressed up in the form of a fable, might invite. In the Roman era, slaves employed to furnish their employers and superiors with the benefits of philosophical teaching were particularly vulnerable to the retribution of an unappreciative student. Given his position, Julian concedes, a slave must "take pains to flatter and cure his master at the same time." The slave-tutor must soothe the effects of his "moral exhortation and instruction" by making his teachings less direct, by wrapping them up in edifying stories. For the Cynic teacher, however, who bases his philosophy in the claim that "he alone is free," this is entirely inappropriate.[77] The Cynic has no need of myths or other such devices that might ease the passage of his moralizing discourse and thereby protect him from any reprisals his advice may prompt. The Cynic has no time for such false-ness, Julian argues. Under Cynic teaching, lessons are rela-tively abrupt—and here we can still see traces of an older, more abrasive Cynicism—though for Julian the target has changed, from an attack on all customs, to an attack on the body. The body in all its distraction becomes something the Roman Cynic learns to "utterly despise" as Julian puts it, and regard as "more deserving to be thrown out than dung."[78]

The true Cynic (as Julian imagines him) learns to con-trol his passions and ensure he will never again be ruled by his "nether regions." He also learns to disregard pub-lic opinion, since the man "who has attained to a life of reason" does not require the guidance of conventional mores.[79] He has transcended them. No longer distracted by the body or by the mob, Julian continues, the Cynic is free to "train his mind on clean, pure and holy thoughts."[80] True followers of Diogenes will affirm with Plato the supe-riority of the soul over the body in which it is confined.[81] The Roman Cynic will do everything he can to step "out-side himself," being assured that "the soul within him is divine."[82] His soul is educated, and as such has begun to realize its potential for divinity, in contrast to those who, by their ignorance, remain "tied to the body" and popu-lar opinion. His soul approaches the freedom promised by philosophy, having been schooled against those who are "subject to false opinion rather than truth."[83] From this exalted position, the ignorant, uneducated subjects of Julian's day were to be pitied, if not despised. Julian submits Cynicism, in other words, to multiple distortions. In recuperating Cynicism, he reverses the Cynic attitude, renders it respectable, and recruits it to the cause of a far more conventional conception of education and philosophy.

Christian Ascetics and Holy Fools

Christian revivals differed from their educated Roman counterparts (who were busy marginalizing street Cynics), since early Christians at first shared the Cynic's subaltern point of view. It was through Christianity that some of the more practical aspects of Cynicism were retained and transformed, where for centuries, as Foucault argues, the "major medium for the Cynic mode of being across Europe" was Christian asceticism.[84] The Christian ascetic lived according to a regime of self-discipline and abstention from indulgence that bore resemblance to the extreme, courageous destitution of the ancient Cynic. Many Cynic "themes, attitudes, and forms of behavior" were passed on in all but name through the intermediaries of Christian asceticism and monasticism. Of particular note are the mendicant orders, the Franciscans and Dominicans (or "Hounds of the Lord" as they were known)—those who, "stripping themselves of everything" went "bare foot to call men to look to their salvation."[85] This emphasis on ascetic destitution was, as Foucault suggests, a "particularly lively, intense, and strong practice in all the efforts at reform which were opposed to the Church, its institutions, its increasing wealth, and its moral laxity." These traditions of "anti-institutional [Christian] Cynicism" lasted at least as far as the Reformation.[86]

Sloterdijk also recognizes this Christian inheritance, but is damning in his summation of it. Christian ascetics effectively ruined the word: "To call [Diogenes] an ascetic," Sloterdijk argues, "would be incorrect because of the false undertones the word asceticism has assumed through a thousand-year-long masochistic misunderstanding." Though some scholars might balk at this sweeping characterization, what Sloterdijk is effectively arguing here is that, with Christianity, asceticism became associated with self-mortification, a position that could not be further removed from the Cynic affirmation of bodily existence. Sloterdijk believes that we have to "rid the word of its Christian connotations to rediscover its fundamental meaning."[87] Presumably, we would once more be able to appreciate the "shameless asceticism" of the ancient Cynic, where Cynic shamelessness did not simply teach "If it feels good, do it."[88] Rather, the Cynic ascetic "trained to transgress."[89] Foucault makes a similar point when he claims that "we should distinguish the future Christian humility" from Cynic humiliation. As argued in an earlier chapter: the Cynic "asserts his sovereignty, his mastery through these tests of humiliation, whereas Christian humiliation, or rather, humility, is a renunciation of oneself."[90] Broadly speaking, Christian ascetics are blamed here for weakening Cynic philosophy by embarking upon a course of action that diminished and humbled the ascetic practitioner. As an overall characterization this might hold water, but there are also notable examples of Christian ascetics who could be remarkably assertive.

Recent studies exploring affinities between Cynicism and the origins of Christianity generally bear out Sloterdijk's claim that there was an overall softening of the Cynic tradition.[91] It has been argued, with a great deal of qualification, that Jesus was not simply a "Jewish Peasant"[92] but also a Cynic, along with John the Baptist and Paul. It is claimed that they incorporated elements from Cynic philosophy into their teaching or, to ease the burden of proof, displayed a series of remarkably similar traits—including a commitment to poverty and itinerancy, an elevation of practice over theory, and a rejection of Hellenistic-Roman hierarchies of power and patronage. This Cynic influence was potentially transmitted by way of its impact on Hellenistic Judaism,[93] but also possibly by direct experience of street Cynics in Lower Galilee.[94] Important differences have been pointed out, with Jesus and his followers credited with a level of "collective discipline" and a capacity for "communal action" for which the ancient Cynic apparently had no aptitude.[95] Though a shared tendency to "subversive wisdom" is thought to underpin both traditions, with the early followers of Jesus committing to a marginal existence, resisting dominant social norms from positions of weakness in ways that bear close analogy to Cynic tactics,[96] it is notable that the version of Cynicism dealt with in these studies is largely obscenity-free. There is a tendency in such work to downplay the significance of Cynic shamelessness, with scholarly interest in Jesus and his associates "unlikely to focus on stories of Cynics' spitting, farting, or defecating."[97] From the position of a biblical scholar this is understandable; there are other, potentially more apt associations between Cynicism and early Christianity deserving of attention. The accusation that such commentators downplay Cynic shamelessness has been rebuffed by the claim that those who persist in identifying Cynicism with its most scandalous acts are guilty of a kind of juvenile interest or puerile fascination. Surely, so the argument goes, the cleaner, less scatological Cynic inheritances are just as deserving of the name.[98] In responding to this accusation, one might argue that it is undoubtedly true that certain Cynic episodes retain their capacity to entertain and amuse. But this emphasis on the Cynic body and its excretory and sexual functions derives from an appreciation of how, as a site of regulation, the body is expected to reflect and uphold the judgmental operations of a broader social

Emphasis on the Cynic body and its excretory and sexual functions derives from an appreciation of how, as a site of regulation, the body is expected to reflect and uphold the judgmental operations of a broader social order.

order.[99] This order defines the boundaries within which the body must operate, as it stipulates what can be taken in, what may be expelled, and the manner in which it may be done.[100] Cynic practice interrupts those prohibitions by focusing attention on substances that pass regularly into or out of the body and on how they are regulated and prescribed. In so doing, the Cynic places the body at the center of his or her political practice. If this interest in bodily functions had already been given up by the time of Jesus, it would be a major loss for the Cynic tradition. And yet, if Emperor Julian's disgust at the street Cynics of his day is a reliable indicator, Cynics retained their commitment to shameless and offensive behavior for some centuries still.

Symeon the Fool

Engagement with a more obscene Diogenes can be found in Christian writing, particularly during the fourth century. This engagement was part of a wider attempt to absorb pagan philosophy within the intellectual and educational traditions of Christianity.[101] In the same century that Julian presented his idealized Diogenes as an alternative to Christian asceticism, Julian's Christian opponents used Diogenes to help sell asceticism to a suspicious Christian elite. Diogenes was either put forward as a (once again sanitized) moral exemplar—a proponent of the undeviating, unpretentious, unadorned life—or rejected for his Cynic pride, puerility, and shameless behavior in order to distinguish Christian asceticism from its closest pagan equivalent. This reception of Cynicism was swept up in a broader debate between pagans and Christians over which community was "the legitimate heir of Greco-Roman educational and philosophical traditions."[102] Diogenes was maintained as a stock character in both. Owing much to these developments, one account of a Cynic-like Christian ascetic stands out. This is the *Life of Symeon the Fool* composed by the Cypriot bishop Leontius of Neapolis in the seventh century. In the Christian tradition, the "Holy Fool" offers an exemplary case of a more strident, scandalous, outward-facing asceticism, where Symeon appears far removed from the domesticated monk envisaged by Sloterdijk.

Like Diogenes, Symeon is encountered secondhand, through the *Life* composed nearly a century after his death. It has been argued that in constructing his account of Symeon, Leontius is influenced by and draws from the anecdotes of Diogenes; the *chreiai* or popular sayings attributed to Diogenes that were still very much part of the rhetorical curriculum of Hellenistic and Late Antique schools.[103] They were assembled alongside thousands of other sayings attributed to famous figures, forming the building blocks of a rhetorical training in which teachers developed their students' oratorical skills. The intention was to transmit aristocratic values, where the *chreiai* relating to Diogenes functioned as moral discussion points

rather than as examples to be emulated; they "helped ensure social conformity" rather than subvert it.[104] Relatively
well-known, then, these sayings and anecdotes provided
not simply a model for Leontius's account of Symeon but
a common framework through which his account would
have been understood.

Leontius's *Life of Symeon* is stylistically odd, divided
between a syntactically complex narration of Symeon's
early life in the first part, and a collection of bawdy anecdotes in the second. Relating Symeon's later years, this
second part is written in a colloquial style that would presumably have appealed to a more general audience. The
dual (or diglossic) character of the text has caused some
debate and speculation over its composition, with the suggestion that Leontius merely pasted the second half into
his account from another source.[105] Whatever its prove-
nance, it is significant that this text does not subsume the
uncouth side of Symeon's Christian Cynicism by dressing
it up in more refined language. Leontius does frequently
apologize for what he narrates, and begs the reader's indulgence. His verbose first half also frames the scandalous
second half, preparing the reader by explaining that the life
it depicts was the outcome of years of self-mortification
and pious withdrawal. But Leontius does not divide
Symeon's Cynicism into its acceptable and deviant parts,
as Julian submitted the Cynics of his day to systematic
cleansing.[106]

Having spent many years in the desert, Symeon is said to have entered town with a dead dog in tow. He threw nuts at women in church, ate enormous quantities of beans, defecated in the street, and made a general nuisance of himself. The allusions to Cynicism are pretty obvious: "In attaching Symeon to the dog, Leontius attaches Symeon to the Cynic tradition, both linguistically and metaphorically."[107] The eating of beans also bears analogy to Cynic tradition, where Diogenes was said to consume vast quantities for the wind it produced.[108] Though Symeon attracted the ire of the local population, he bore his persecutors with equanimity. It is claimed that through "his inventiveness, he nearly put an end to sinning in the whole city."[109] Symeon somehow managed to convert heretics, Jews, prostitutes, and actors. He was nonetheless hostile to those who might follow him, and whenever his holiness was recognized, he would do his best to dispel the impression it gave. Living in a small hut, wearing an old cloak, "suffering neither from cold, hunger nor heat," Symeon appears to have achieved the kind of bodily self-discipline identified with Diogenes.[110]

Although Symeon was said to have the ability to heal others—a typical attribute of early Christian holy men—he nonetheless "seems to afflict people with physical problems as often as he cures them."[111] Again, this appears to mirror the conception of Diogenes as an aggressive benefactor. Embodying his teaching in acts of apparent madness, Symeon deliberately provoked righteous indignation, and encouraged the beatings and derision he received. Symeon's scandalous, shameless behavior subverted norms of common decency and played with the expectations of what a Christian ascetic practitioner should look and feel like, as he ran naked, for instance, into the women's bathhouse. This led him to appear, in Leontius's words, as if he were a kind of "defilement, a sort of poison, and an impediment to the virtuous life," though he was actually "most pure, just as a pearl which has travelled through slime unsullied."[112]

As this brief account demonstrates, there is considerable affinity between Symeon and the ancient Cynics, though a good dose of Christian piety nonetheless intrudes upon his Cynicism. It is perhaps significant that the dog Symeon drags into the city is dead, suggesting that Symeon has somehow exceeded ancient Cynicism. Insofar as Symeon imitates Diogenes, this might even be part of his disguise, so that Symeon's outward behavior is a ruse that conceals his inner sanctity. Symeon only appears to live in accord with nature, like the Cynic. Actually, his life is underpinned by its commitment to Christian virtue. Precisely because of his virtue Symeon could not be 'defiled' by the women he encountered in the bathhouse; his genitals had already been exorcised in the desert and thereby freed of the "nuisance of erections."[113] Beneath it all, Symeon is committed to moral instruction, conversion to Christianity, and perhaps most oddly of all, social and religious conformity. In describing Symeon's life, Leontius is not advocating that others imitate his example. Symeon is used to reveal and comment on the hypocrisies of urban life and thereby deliver a characteristically Christian message of social critique and redemption.[114]

To further develop the distinction between Symeon and the Cynic he resembled, it is worth noting that in his role as holy fool Symeon challenged social norms only after having learned to live without them through his years in isolation. Given his prior training involving a typically Christian mortification of the flesh, Symeon could declare, so Leontius reports, that neither did he have a body, nor had he entered among bodies.[115] The ancient Cynic, by contrast, pretended to no inner sanctity, and battled with social norms from within society, acutely feeling the presence of his or her body in relation to the social conventions that conditioned it. This was a more uncertain assignment, since it did not resource itself from appeal to God, nor did it draw from another already-contrived mode of existence, which for Symeon was the already well-known and well-established life of the desert monk. Cynic practice, by contrast, labored toward an as yet unlived mode of being, a future marked by its radical alterity.

DRAIN THE BARREL: EARLY MODERN MALCONTENTS

The reception of Cynicism splits further into competing, mutually incompatible elements as Diogenes makes his appearance on "the cultural stage of the Renaissance."[1] The rediscovery of Greek literature during that period, including the translation of Laertius's work into Latin by around 1433,[2] provided new sources through which ancient Cynicism might be understood. To put it in Cynic terms, the Renaissance afforded a proper "dog's breakfast" of rival interpretations. There was not a complete break between medieval and Renaissance images of Cynicism, since "the Renaissance continued to feed off medieval writings."[3] It inherited the ambivalent attitude toward Cynicism of pagan and early Christian writers, where in the latter case positions ranged between Jerome's celebration of Cynic self-restraint in the late fourth century, to Augustine's incredulity in the early fifth century before the "ridiculous indecency of the Cynics."[4] Long departed by the time of the Renaissance, however, was the need to defend an idealized Cynicism from base Cynicisms associated with the street. Since the fifth or sixth century by some accounts, Cynic sects were no longer active.[5] Medieval theologians and Renaissance humanists could appeal to Cynic philosophy "as a secular model for rejection of the materialism of this life," without having to first define themselves in opposition to the uncomfortable, all-too-material example of the mendicant Cynic preacher.[6]

In places, Diogenes appears in medieval literature as a friend of poverty, virtue, and self-mastery, offering a pagan equivalent to the poverty of the apostles. He is taken to exemplify a form of resolute piety that is almost destined to be misunderstood by the ignorant. For example, John of Wales, a thirteenth-century Franciscan theologian, describes Diogenes's virtues at length. These include firmness of soul, constancy, self-control, the ability to suppress the vices and other cravings, frankness, avoidance of flattery, and compassion for the sufferings of others.[7] This kind of interpretation extends to the Renaissance; in his fifteenth-century treatise on education, the Renaissance poet Maffeo Vegio offers Diogenes as an example to the young, that they may study philosophy "not for any speculative understanding it might give them, but in order to have an immediate intuition of the just and honest aims one should have in life, and of how these may be achieved."[8]

Later in the century, the humanist Robert Gaguin can be found sending King Charles VIII of France the apocryphal letters of Crates, remarking how astonishing it is "that a Cynic who lived centuries before our Lord" could display so much "that is in keeping with Christian law."[9]

As an oddly pious Cynicism was put to work, Cynic shamelessness was explained away. One approach was to claim that the occasional vulgarity of ancient Cynicism was the product of the ancients' generally simpler and humbler way of life.[10] Alternatively, Cynic discharges could be explained on medical grounds: if Diogenes, "a person of great severity and continence, had several times made use of Venus," it was because he felt "the retention of his seed was obnoxious and damaging to him."[11] This accorded with medical advice, that semen should be expelled for reasons of health. Other Renaissance writers were more cautious, suggesting, for instance, that Diogenes still showed too great an interest in the body, and, together with all pagan philosophy, was at best only a pale anticipation of those who would come to know Christ.[12] Dominican and Jesuit preachers in the sixteenth and seventeenth centuries would nonetheless continue to draw from Cynic folklore to illustrate their sermons, focusing in particular on Diogenes's condemnation of flatterers, his temperance, sobriety, and voluntary poverty.[13]

Cynicism was also mobilized for its opposite function. It figured not only as an exemplar of proto-Christian piety, but also in efforts to denounce aberrant Christian sects. In this context, Cynic associations were deemed sufficiently toxic to reject a religious sect out of hand. The "heresy of the Beghards and Turlupins, who claimed that nothing that is natural should be able to embarrass us," was thereby condemned. They were dismissed for being "like the Cynics who live as dogs do, naked, and disport the shameful parts of the body."[14] In a dictionary of heresies published in 1569, these two sects, and others, are once more associated with the Cynics, with Cynicism now treated as a heresy in its own right and given a separate entry: "Those carnal and bestial philosophers, who believed that it was acceptable to copulate with women as shamelessly as dog with dog [a reference to Crates and Hipparchia], were imitated by the Waldenses and similar heretics several centuries later ... their debaucheries copied by many, who scorned all authority and blasphemed against sovereign power."[15] Italian Renaissance humanists expanded on such criticisms, declaring that Cynic philosophy had "its roots in a profound self-hatred," and was "the mother of fraud, hypocrisy and vice." The Jesuit polemicist François Garasse dismissed Diogenes as a "self-conceited fool, and an atheist to boot"; if he lived in a barrel, it was only because he was "overfond of wine."[16] Francesco Collio, in his 1622 attempt to determine which pagans were damned and which destined for salvation, submits Diogenes to trial in which all his virtues turn out to be vices.[17] It seems as though the tendentious association drawn by previous figures between Cynicism and Christianity in an attempt to dignify the latter had now come home to roost.

Rabelais

In addition to the pious division in Renaissance literature (resembling a similar division in medieval texts) between those who celebrated Cynic asceticism and those who rejected Cynic shamelessness, the influence of Cynicism on Renaissance authors led to more playful usage.[18] The most notorious example is the bawdy, wine-soaked work of Rabelais, which I consider here in comparative detail. Written in the sixteenth century, his *Gargantua and Pantagruel* is a grotesque comic fantasy recounting the exploits of two giants and their various associates. "Most noble and illustrious drinkers," it begins, "to you, and none else, do I dedicate my writings."[19] Though the intended audience is decidedly highbrow—with the work permeated by cultural references and allusions that only the well-educated would be able to detect—the jesting is deliberately uncouth.

Diogenes makes an appearance in Book 2 of *Gargantua and Pantagruel*. During a visit to Hell he is found strutting about "most pompously, and in great magnificence, with a rich purple gown on him, and a golden sceptre in his right hand."[20] The implication might be that Hell, for Diogenes, would be a place in which he is forced to strut about in such a way (and forced to enjoy it). However, his appearance has been interpreted rather differently as a carnivalesque role-reversal in which power is ridiculed by having its opponent adopt its attire.[21] Given the thickly satirical context of Rabelais's work, it is hard to know quite what to make of this appearance. Diogenes appears once more in the prologue to Book 3, again addressed to "illustrious drinkers" but also "gouty gentlemen"[22]—a disease long associated with the rich. In that prologue Rabelais identifies himself with Diogenes, using the Cynic to frame the book that follows. Despite the obvious significance given to Diogenes (Book 3 was the first to appear under Rabelais's own name, making the decision to associate with the philosopher particularly noteworthy), the exact role of Diogenes in framing that text remains obscure and has been subject to considerable debate.[23] The book has itself been described by one of its foremost experts as "utterly perplexing": "It begins with an ending, ends with a beginning, and contains within it an open-ended quest whose point is never clear and whose telos is indefinitely deferred"; "weighed down by great masses or erudition and interrupted by irreverent digressions—diatribes, anecdotes, and *facetiae* ... the quest never reaches its goal"; "it is hard to know precisely *what* this book is about."[24]

One interpretation is that mention of Diogenes forms part of a deliberate ploy by Rabelais to "bewilder and provoke his readership," unsettling its attachments, upending its expectations, in a Cynic maneuver designed to prepare that audience for an engagement with alterity and the necessary uncertainty that engagement will involve.[25] Rabelais identifies himself with Diogenes in order to prepare the reader for a book that is "deliberately non-systematic."[26] Book 3 can thereby be understood in terms of Cynic "free improvisation." It takes its cue from Diogenes's *modus operandi*, here understood as a "combination of contrariness and humour which subverts and unsettles interpretation, as opposed to providing a method or key."[27]

Diogenes is nonetheless characterized as a friend and associate of educated people, including the illustrious readers of Rabelais. In the prologue, Rabelais adapts the following anecdote from Lucian—and thereby indicates one route by which Cynicism influences his work—which in the original reads:

> When Philip was said to be already on the march,
> all the Corinthians were astir and busy, preparing
> weapons, bringing up stones, underpinning the wall,
> shoring up a battlement and doing various other
> useful jobs. Diogenes saw this, and as he had nothing
> to do—nobody made any use of him—he belted up
> his philosopher's cloak and very busily by himself
> rolled the crock in which, as it happens, he was living
> up and down Cornell Hill. When one of his friends

asked: "Why are you doing that, Diogenes?" he replied: "I'm rolling the crock so as not to be thought the one idle man in the midst of all these workers."[28]

In Rabelais's adaptation of the above anecdote from Lucian, he gives Diogenes books and writing materials, which must be cast aside before the barrel-rolling can begin. This is not the only embellishment, but it is a significant one, since it downplays the hostility to writing and reading that can be found in Laertius's *Lives*, a text well known in the Renaissance.[29] Though Diogenes casts these materials aside, he obviously has them to begin with. Once more, given the satirical context in which it appears, it is hard to know what to make of this addition.[30] Whether Diogenes has become a friend of the educated (which would mean that he has given up his hostility to books and bookish people—that is, to people who look for wisdom in books) or whether he remains hostile in some way, by associating himself with Diogenes in this example, Rabelais offers a humorous commentary on his own writing. He suggests that it might appear just as pointless as Diogenes's barrel-rolling. All it offers is a little comic relief in times of war.

But if Rabelais employs Diogenes as a subversive character and not simply as a comedic buffoon, his own self-consciously absurd activity as a tub-shuffling drink-toting writer carries a more devious message,[31] namely, those who think they are engaged in more serious activities than

If Rabelais employs Diogenes as a subversive character and not simply as a comedic buffoon, his own activity as a tub-shuffling drink-toting writer carries a more devious message.

the barrel-rolling of a light-hearted satirist are the real dupes. They are unable to see the comical side, perhaps even the absurd futility of their own ceaseless labor (lawyers, pettifoggers, hypocrites, and monks are among those named).[32] This is the devious implication, after all, of the barrel-rolling episode; it not only suggests that the frantic efforts to mount defenses in Corinth were unnecessary (since the invasion never materializes) and futile (since the Corinthians would have been unable to withstand an attack had it occurred), it also suggests (and this is where the joke really strikes home) that there is some kind of equivalence between barrel-rolling and other forms of labor. Actually, the barrel might be preferable for those prepared to endure it.

Rabelais invites only those readers prepared to savor him without hesitation or doubt to drink "frankly, freely, and boldly" from his tub, now filled with wine, "for how much soever you shall draw forth at the faucet, so much shall I tun in at the bung." For those who deserve it, his barrel will "remain inexhaustible." To the right kind of drinker, it is a "true cornucopia of merriment and raillery."[33] His book is offered as an enlivening but corrupting draft. Though the barrel is recommended as a source of merriment, the merits of barrel-rolling remain ambivalent. And since all other forms of labor are equivalent to barrel-rolling, their merits remain ambivalent too. Rabelais at one point equates Diogenes's barrel-rolling with the absurd task set for Sisyphus—to roll a large boulder uphill, never to reach the summit—a lesson in futility and endless labor if ever there was one. Here, in suggesting that we achieve little more than Sisyphus, Rabelais seems to anticipate the pessimistic outlook of the modern cynic.[34]

The body figures prominently in *Gargantua and Pantagruel* as a degrading influence, full of farts and whistles. This could be taken as further evidence of the role of Cynicism in Rabelais's work. Such an interpretation might need to distance itself, however, from Bakhtin's influential analysis, which strays toward Cynic themes. According to Bakhtin, Rabelais offers the purest example of "grotesque realism" in literature:[35] "The essential principle of grotesque realism is degradation," Bakhtin claims, "that is, the lowering of all that is high, spiritual, ideal, abstract" to the "sphere of earth and body in their indissoluble unity." Degradation is understood here in a positive sense, where the body achieves cosmic significance as it is reduced to its fundamentals. It is not presented in its "private, egotistical form, severed from the other spheres of life, but as something universal." The materiality of the body, Bakhtin interprets, is "contained not in the biological individual, not in the bourgeois ego, but in the people." This is why the body assumes such grandiose, bloated significance in *Gargantua and Pantagruel*. It comes to signify the basic oneness of all people, united by a shared materiality, by a common earthly existence characterized by the overlapping of life, death, and rebirth. For Bakhtin, this typifies the "utopian aspect" of grotesque realism. It also defines its comedic function, where "the people's laughter," the laughter of bawdy jokes and marketplace jostling, is once more admired in its baseness: "Laughter degrades and materializes."[36] Laughter attacks the "narrow-minded and stupid seriousness" of all higher forms of understanding, and "frees human consciousness, thought, and imagination for new potentialities." In Rabelais, the grotesque "discloses the potentiality of an entirely different world, of another order, another way of life." That potentiality is revealed to the intellect not in ideals or visions, but in a grotesque "bodily awareness of another world," a world no longer ordered according to a false understanding of its nature.[37] Aspects of Cynic practice may be found in the above description, where Cynicism also renders private matters public. It too degrades and materializes, placing the body at the center of its practice as it demonstrates the possibility of another life. In a similar way, that life can only emerge through a Cynic deconstruction of all prevailing concepts that direct our existence and condition our being. Yet Cynicism avoids the cloying optimism of Bakhtin's analysis, which places such hope in a "people" or folk culture to be admired for its "degradation" and baseness. It avoids a point of view that bases its optimism in the assumed, rejuvenating presence of nature, to which "earthy" people provide access. Cynic degradations do not

Cynicism avoids the cloying optimism of Bakhtin's analysis, which places such hope in a "people" or folk culture to be admired for its "degradation" and baseness.

halt in this manner to erect alternative ideals, humanist or otherwise.

Bakhtin strays close to another key Cynic theme when he argues that in *Gargantua and Pantagruel* there is "no world of interiority. ... There is nothing that cannot adequately be made public."[38] Subsequent interpreters have continued this line of argument: Rabelais's text is "remarkably unlike modern literature, and Montaigne's *Essays*, in its neglect of the internal psychological workings of the self. All that persons are in Rabelais is expressed through action, dialogue and the body, the innermost workings of which are put on display."[39] Once more there are potential links to Cynic philosophy, which externalizes everything that ought to be kept private. Deliberately shallow, performing the operations of body and self on the same external plane, the Cynic elevates nothing and conceals little. The very features Cynicism shares with Rabelais are also the distinguishing features that separate both from modern literature. Preoccupied with the inner workings of the self, modern literature generates a pretense of psychological depth, or so a Cynic might claim, with readers retreating into its characteristic mode of enjoyment: private contemplation. For the Cynic, Rabelais could offer a way of undermining the culture of modern bourgeois literature. Within that culture, literature operates as a moral technology, or governmental device; it helps construct the subjective frameworks within which the educated are trapped, though they do not perceive their imprisonment as such.[40] If Rabelais were somehow freed from the grasp of his various interpreters and specialists, he might help rupture the sensibilities that modern literature supports. With its focus on individual character formation within the complexity and richness of lived experience, modern literature dignifies the liberal humanism of the educated by conjuring in them a sense of depth and moral seriousness. As it does so, it conveys the experience of a moral existence without necessarily specifying a moral code. This renders the subjective frameworks it constructs adaptable to changing political circumstance. As Terry Eagleton once put it, modern literature figures educated subjectivity as "an end in itself, which works, apparently, all by itself, and which is its own justification."[41] As the educated brood over the very meaning of life and enjoy "the rich inwardness of [their] being" as they find it reflected in literature,[42] they may adapt to otherwise perturbing circumstances, and by peacefully living within them, assent to the operations of increasingly ruinous political and economic orders. The educated will continue to adapt so long as the arts and humanities survive in some form, so long as art galleries can still be visited, plays enjoyed, and reading groups convened. The educated may express alarm at times and sign petitions, rally even, for the outlook of the educated person is increasingly an anguished one; but they will remain fundamentally undisturbed so long as the reflective imbecility of their educated subjectivity is provided for. Effectively, that subjective position declares: "If people like us can still exist in a society like this, then surely there is still hope." A Cynic use of Rabelais might undermine this bleached out humanistic outlook by emphasizing the contorted physiognomy of the educated person.

For Bakhtin, however, Rabelais's representation of the human being as "completely external" serves very different ends. By presenting the human being in this way, by constructing characters that lack any spiritual interiority, Rabelais achieves the dissolution of individual "biographical time" in the "apersonal time" of "historical growth and cultural progress." Rabelais exceeds "the sealed-off sequence of an individual life" and gains access to "the all-embracing common life of the human race."[43] In Bakhtin's reading, if Rabelais undermines the individualism of the modern bourgeois subject, he nonetheless flatters the implicit humanism of the educated person. For Bakhtin, Rabelais provides another point of access through literature to our common humanity.

The radical intent of specific bodily acts represented in *Gargantua and Pantagruel* are also difficult to interpret in terms of their Cynic content. Benefiting from the scope afforded by fantasy rather than the very real and urgent contexts a Cynic might have to negotiate, Rabelais offers a far more diverse range of perverse scenarios and shameless acts, ranging from "How Gargantua did eat up six Pilgrims in a Sallad" only to spit them out and send them away upon a stream of urine,[44] to "How Pantagruel likewise with his Farts begat Little Men."[45] It is hard to judge whether these scenarios are to be understood as Cynic acts of some kind represented in a fantasy context, or if they should be understood as being perverse and offensive (for some) in a different kind of way. In either case, these examples remain fictive, and so the Cynicism of this work (such as it is) remains of a literary kind. Norms are upended from within the discourse of the educated, rather than by confrontation with individuals modeling a different mode of life through their behavior. In this literary context, we encounter the clever manipulation of educated cultural norms, rather than their inversion through the aggressive, uncouth presence of the street Cynic who looks, acts, sounds, and smells a little off. This is not to diminish the subversive potential of a more literary Cynicism, nor is it to deny the dangers Rabelais faced as an author working in a context where men (including men known to Rabelais) were burned for their books.[46] Given this context, Rabelais's invocation of Diogenes has been interpreted as a brave appeal to Cynic humor, an insistence on his part that Cynic laughter must prevail even in the darkest times.[47] But it is worth noticing once more what Cynicism had given up. It had long been engulfed by (and modified through) Christian ascetic practices on the one hand, and, as Rabelais demonstrates, by literary production, on the other.

Early Modern Malcontents

The process of displacement and adjustment by which ancient Cynicism was transformed (which began with its first Greek and Roman interpreters and detractors as recounted above) was further compounded in the early modern period by what has been described as the "vernacularization" of Cynicism. Though the fate of Cynicism, its entire history, is bedeviled by the absence of foundational texts or doctrines, it is argued that during the early modern period Cynicism was rendered "unusually open to topical, popular, or vernacular interpretative pressures." Consequently, the meaning of Cynicism continued to "expand well past its classical parameters."[48] In the English context, the Cynic was recast as some kind of "railer, misanthrope, melancholic, or malcontent."[49] It is here, perhaps, that Cynicism began to acquire its modern association with a jaded negativity.

Cynic folklore was widely disseminated through translations of ancient texts, newly compiled collections of ancient sayings (such as Erasmus's *Apophthegms*), as well as vernacular collections, emblem books, encyclopedias, and miscellanies intended both for a reading public and for use in the school curriculum.[50] The enduring prestige of rhetoric, which would retain its cultural and curricular position of influence up until the mid-seventeenth century, meant that students were still exposed as a matter of routine to Cynic anecdotes and sayings. In positive assessments, Diogenes's frank speech or parrhesia was not understood to represent a challenge to the student's training in eloquence. Indeed, Diogenes was more often depicted as a wise "counselor" and model of courtly persuasion, courageously advising rather than berating those in power. The potential audience of Cynic speech was redefined so that it addressed the sovereign rather than the anonymous urban crowd.[51] This fresh emphasis on the continuing potential of the (respectable) Cynic to speak truth to power, insistence on the idea that a bold and courageous Cynic-like sovereign self could serve as an agent of positive change at court, might well reflect what has been described as a "fantasy" of sovereign frankness. This was a "compensatory response to the development of a cash and credit economy," an attempt to resurrect old techniques rendered defunct by the early development of a capitalist economy where cash, and no longer the sovereign, is king.[52]

But rhetoric also provided the materials for damning assessments of Cynicism that did not allow it a role at court. Here, once more, we encounter a vehemently negative assessment that accompanies the positive estimation of Cynicism just introduced. During the sixteenth and early seventeenth centuries, rhetorical training still owed much to Cicero. Where portrayals of Diogenes were negative, they carried forward Cicero's own judgment in which he deplored the Cynics for their lack of seemliness, honor, consideration, and civility. Diogenes served in such negative accounts as an example of what the good, well-mannered student must avoid. He was offered up as a case of what happens as a result of a *lack* of self-control—in short, a loss of verbal powers (via a lost eloquence) and a loss of social status. In an effort to "demonstrate the importance of propriety to effective speech, a propriety as much physical as it is verbal," this reading contributed to a "low view" of Diogenes in which he is depicted as nothing but a "sour misanthrope." Here Diogenes becomes the "despised antitype" of the eloquent humanist. In contrast to the humanist's commitment to active public life, the Cynic is now reconfigured as "the solitary, melancholic, malcontent in retirement." This Cynicism is presented as an affliction of the privileged, rather than the social outcast, where the melancholia it produces is a vice imputed to "leisured gentlemen."[53] A depleted gentlemanly Cynicism was understood by its detractors to be a consequence of decline and enfeeblement, suffered by those who have retreated from public life—Cynicism is no longer the affliction of the ignorant, unenlightened, and dispossessed.

This negative assessment prepared the way for writers such as Shakespeare to expand on the figure of the moribund Cynic. Beginning with Shakespeare's lesser-known play *Timon of Athens*, it has been argued that the Cynic is denigrated here as nothing better than a sour misanthrope who combines "disillusionment with human viciousness."[54] In that play, the false Cynic Apemantus and the misanthropic Timon testify to a larger intellectual and social malaise, where their ineffectiveness "only reflects the more general paralysis affecting the social institutions and leadership of Timon's Athens." This depiction of irredeemable social decay has been interpreted as an integral part of Shakespeare's overall "rebuttal of the more grandiose claims" that are made on behalf of persuasive speech, namely, "that the trained man of eloquence is an agent of civilization who helps raise mankind out of its former beastliness."[55] It is also claimed that the play pillories the idea that self-mastery (including Cynic self-mastery) can be the root of a radical, transformative politics.[56] Classical training, rhetoric, and eloquence (even Cynic parrhesia and self-sufficiency) appear to have become obsolete in a degenerating social order, where money (and debt) is now the only agent of persuasion, and a most degraded one at that.[57] Cynicism is here viewed as part of that decline, rather than offering a way out. Indeed, the false Cynic Apemantus may be interpreted as an active, vengeful participant in Timon's downfall. Eventually, through "silence, complicity, and inaction," he allows Timon "to advance unimpeded toward doom."[58] This is the role we might indeed attribute to the modern cynic, who is silently complicit in the social, political, and environmental catastrophes he or she bemoans. Still, the modern cynic is perhaps not as willfully, consciously, and intentionally involved in that process of decline as Apemantus appears to be.

A slightly different emphasis has been given in relation to *King Lear*, where Shakespeare does not denounce Cynicism, but demonstrates the complexity of its "composite" character.[59] In *King Lear*, Shakespeare shows how easily Cynic parrhesia may be reduced to "the mere antics of a parasite-jester who has renounced all claims to seriousness."[60] In his depiction of the bitter fool, Shakespeare suggests that Cynic candor must inevitably result in "communicative failure" and "critical inefficiency."[61] Shakespeare's Fool is noteworthy for himself drawing attention to these inevitable failings in a display of "knowing irony, announcing his critical impotence at precisely the moment when he is being most incisive and critically forceful."[62] Although this can be taken as an argument against his Cynicism, this gesture might also be understood as prototypically Cynical, insofar as Cynic critique begins with a rhetorical gesture that casts doubt on its claim to legitimacy and on its likely effectiveness within the current order. This is how Cynicism sidesteps those who would seek to instrumentalize it, those who would put it to use within the very frameworks it seeks to overthrow.

Shakespeare's younger contemporary, the poet and satirist John Marston, offers another example of this early modern cynicism, though in a more strident, personally avowed form. Marston openly identifies himself as a cynic (and here we drop to the lowercase) of the railing, misanthropic sort. This cynicism has given up its courtly truth-telling and embraced a mode of critique that was as vicious as it was self-defeating. That, at least, is one interpretation of Marston's 1599 *Scourge of Villainie*, which attacks conventions of decorum and civility while refusing to offer itself as a principled alternative, or pretending that it speaks from a position of virtue or higher truth.[63] As one contemporary described Marston: "Hee is the wheele of a well-couched fire-worke; that flies out on all sides, not without scorching it selfe."[64] Perhaps unsurprisingly, the *Scourge* had a mixed reception, including the following abrupt dismissal, which opens the introduction to the 1925 Bodley Head edition:

> *The Scourge of Villainie* is not a book to be read for pleasure of amusement. It is neither great literature nor even great satire. Its lines are unusually turgid, allusions are most difficult to follow, and the whole, even for Elizabethan satire, is very liberally

"bescumbered." But, for all that, neither the *Scourge* nor its author can be neglected by anyone who wishes to understand the mentality of English writers at the close of the sixteenth century.[65]

In the estimation of more recent and sympathetic critique, we might still hear in Marston's "querulous tone ... the displaced intellectuals of the Elizabethan and Jacobean era discovering their own uselessness to the social and political order." This discovery with its attendant frustration, if not feeling of powerlessness, is what spurred satirists such as Marston to "even freer and less decorous speech"—that is to say, to deliberately offensive writing that testifies to its own "ineffectiveness" to heal or elevate, as much as it reveals in the object of its attacks the "monstrous condition" of the cultured, chattering classes.[66] Though the educated would nurture for some centuries yet the idea that classical training could elevate and protect, this fond illusion has long been accompanied by growing unease, if not a sense of betrayal. Satirists and detractors such as Marston demonstrate that they can testify to such corruption—to the failure of the culture of educated people to deliver a more humane society—only by implicating themselves in its breakdown. And so, it would seem that if Shakespeare's rebuttal of the necessarily elevating effects of eloquence and Marston's self-defeating tirade against the conceit of his class can be understood as Cynic acts in their own right, there might well be a literary role for Cynicism. Against any operationalization of Cynicism as an excuse for greater experimentation in literature of a risqué, ribald, jaw-dropping variety—as a vehicle for more literary barrel-rolling as if it were a sport—a more debased literary Cynicism reveals itself here, in the *Scourge* most of all, as it proceeds to bite its own tail.

UNCHAIN THE SUN: ENLIGHTENED PHILOSOPHERS AND LIBERTINES

The Enlightenment marks the high-water mark of Cynic co-option. To the list of mutually competing elements that included saints, holy fools, and malcontents can now be added philosophes and libertines. Despite its creative adoption, however, Cynicism would also give way to parody, and eventually to rejection. The decline of rhetoric is partly to blame. As rhetoric no longer underpinned the school curriculum, the Cynics were reduced to literary characters of a "rigidly satiric and predetermined type."[1] Rhetorical training had long kept Cynic anecdotes alive, in a sense, as part of a wider training in eloquence and persuasive speech. Without the continual revival of Cynicism in that form, the Cynic began to appear as a relic, no longer relevant to the present, perhaps even at odds with the newly arrived-at self-understanding of modern thinkers who were keen to distinguish themselves from all that is primitive, uncivilized, and resistant to "improvement." Though the value of Cynic interventions had previously been recognized as a useful source of provocation, in early modernity the licensed transgression of the Cynic at court was recast, where a Cynic attitude—in the melancholic, railing early modern form—comes to be understood as representing nothing more than "unreflective hostility" to civilized life.[2] Cynicism arrives in modernity having lost the "dignity" and assumed positivity its absorption within the rhetorical curriculum once conveyed. As such it could be ignored by modern curricula and subsequently marginalized by modern historians of philosophy as irrelevant.[3] With the declining influence of Cynicism as a philosophical and literary tradition, the old self-affirming contrast between venerable and base Cynicisms finally disappears. What remains is the shallow counterpart of a once-lauded Cynicism, namely, the dismissed and by now dimly remembered specter of street Cynicism in opposition to which it was previously defined. That shallow figuration extends to the present as a general label for dejection, negativity, and malcontent. Modern cynicism retains this vague, dismissive association with lower forms of life.

In modernity, cynicism can now also be opposed to education, from which it is finally separated. The idea that cynicism might have anything "useful" to contribute to education as it once did in rhetorical training begins to look odd with the decline of the latter. Far from being a potential beneficiary of cynic input, modern education (standing for hope and improvement) is viewed as if it were in a battle against the forces of cynicism or negativity.[4] This would be an interesting contest if cynicism had not been drained of its vitality and radicalism by way of its prior co-option. Education and cynicism are now treated as opposing forces only because the latter can no longer threaten the former. As I argue elsewhere, this positing of education as a solution to cynicism (by those who must fail on a daily basis to realize the promise of educational fulfillment) is itself a cynical arrangement. It is a prototypical example of cynicism in its reduced modern form.[5] I should admit that here my understanding of modern cynicism is perhaps a little heterodox: according to this interpretation, cynicism in its most duplicitous modern configuration is not so much the consequence of detached negativity or a loss of faith as it is the effect of residual attachments to education, emancipation, liberty, and so forth. Pervasive and well protected, this cynicism is produced for the love of education and the educated person, for the love of what educated people represent.

This point can be illustrated by considering how one might read George Lyttelton's 1765 *Dialogue* between Plato and Diogenes—a political and philosophical commentary written from the perspective of a British statesman, peer, and patron of the arts. In that dialogue, so it has been argued, modern cynicism is represented in a transitional form.[6] The role played by this particular Diogenes appears to anticipate the disposition of the modern "insider cynic," who believes that the "ultimate motives of human action are self-interest and the quest for power"[7] and deals with his or her professional context in those terms. Unlike the cynicism of the powerful, which "pays lip service to the conventional values and moralities of the ruled" and is relatively discreet in its manipulation of others, the cynicism of the insider cynic (said to be particularly common in "alienated middlemen") provides "a precious glimpse into the appalling processes of real power."[8] In Lyttelton's *Dialogue*, Diogenes is beginning to exude such traits, and offers such a glimpse of a future cynicism—our cynicism.

Although modern cynicism undoubtedly takes this form (and migrates from it too, producing tycoons and rulers such as Donald Trump),[9] I would argue the equally distorted figure of Plato in Lyttelton's *Dialogue* also represents a dominant though decidedly more elusive tendency in modern cynicism. In Lyttelton's *Dialogue*, Diogenes castigates Plato for accommodating himself to power in his attempts to politely counsel those who govern nations and convey upon them the benefits of philosophy. In so doing, Diogenes points to the very different cynicism, or professional duplicity, of his opponent:

> You seem to think that the business of philosophy is *to polish men into slaves*; but I say, it is to teach them

to assert, with an untamed and generous spirit, their independence and freedom. You profess to instruct those who want to *ride* their fellow-creatures, how to do it with an easy and gentle rein; but I would have them thrown off, and trampled under the feet of all their deluded or insulted equals, on whose backs they have mounted. Which of us two is the truest friend to mankind?[10]

From Plato's perspective, his politeness is "merely strategic and instrumental for his larger philosophic aims," where "an 'honest and prudent complaisance' is simply the best way for a philosopher to intervene effectively into the lives of others."[11] Though Plato's (Lyttelton's) response has not been analyzed as such, I claim that it follows the typical formula of the liberal, educated cynic. This is the self-deluding, self-ennobling dream of the university academic in particular, who is forever "strategic" in his or her interventions, arguing that it is necessary and prudent to consort with government and other influential agencies in the hope that such careful maneuvering will help loosen (though not break) the reins of power. It is the logic of their studious academic compliance with agencies and systems they are otherwise professionally trained to doubt. This species of academic, liberal-minded cynicism is hard to spot, since it is cloaked by good feeling and claims to beneficence. Its status is also built, rather oddly, on its disavowal of other more obvious cynicisms. It is based on the assumption, first of all, that modern cynicism is a feature of outright hypocrisy (the cynicism of those without scruples) or lack of faith (the cynicism of those given overly to pessimism), or second, that it is a product of disempowerment (the affliction of those in need of the uplifting influence of more education, often seen as a precursor to more meaningful engagement with the democratic process). It has been argued that during the process of its early modern "vernacularization," the educated elite would indeed at times associate Cynicism with the insurrectional potential and dangerous "stupidity" of the herd. This was perhaps itself a crucial transition point, where the educated at their most hopeful began to deny their association with what is today rather dismissively called "mass cynicism."[12] Education in the modern sense—as universal enabler, if not human right—can now be seen as its antidote.

Enlightenment Cynics

For a final take on the ancient tradition of Cynicism, one that toyed again with its positive, disruptive potential, it is necessary to travel from the English context to that of the French Enlightenment, where writers such as Rousseau, Diderot, and Sade were lured once more and in their own idiosyncratic ways by the attractions of Cynic philosophy. In this context, Diogenes was relatable because Enlightenment philosophers associated him with a commitment to reason, their highest authority. Diogenes (according to this particular idealization) pursued the consequences of reason fearlessly, heedless of the restraints of tradition. It is argued that this reading formed "the basis for the Enlightenment philosopher's sympathy for the Cynic." It allowed the Cynic to function as an effective stand-in for Enlightenment ideals such as "freedom from prejudice," "the separation of morality from religious constraints," "cosmopolitanism," "the open criticism of secular and religious authorities," and, most distorting of all with regard to Cynic tradition, "the autonomy of the individual."[13] This was a tradition and uptake of Cynic themes from which English writers, such as Edmund Burke, would later recoil in support of their own distinctly pinched political outlook.[14] The Enlightenment can be seen as marking the final, major appeal to Cynicism as a philosophy in its own right, before Cynic philosophy was largely jettisoned and overtaken by its modern vernacular understanding.

Cynicism enjoyed a complex revival: despite its contribution to a potentially disruptive radicalism, the Enlightenment uptake of Cynicism was also instrumental to its further weakening as a militant philosophy.[15] Though Cynicism had its attractions, in that it would give Enlightenment reason more bite, those who adopted it had to contend with the countercritique that they had taken their Cynicism too far and abandoned reason as a consequence. Hence, as Cynic ideas were adapted to a critique of public norms and traditions, the most scurrilous and scatological elements of Cynicism were carefully excised (or in the case of Sade, put to very different use). It has been suggested that Cynicism was eventually so "flattened" by its co-option by the work of Enlightenment that, as a philosophy, it was finally, and most conclusively, diminished to insignificance.[16] This reduction in the power of Cynic philosophy to scandalize and upset was followed by its condemnation by Hegel for being "theoretically unfit"—a nonsensical rationale from the Cynic perspective—and its consequent marginalization by the dour standards of newly professionalized philosophy.[17] If Cynicism lived on by way of the Enlightenment, it persisted only in what it helped engender, namely, Enlightenment-inspired critique. And here the legacy of Enlightenment "Cynicism" might be considered to be overwhelmingly negative, insofar as it helped form a critical consciousness that respected no boundaries, and which would as a result eventually undermine its own foundations. As Sloterdijk argues, modern cynicism can be viewed as the distant ancestor of Enlightenment critique. It can be understood as the "final, melancholic resting place of an exhausted critical consciousness" that has at last consumed itself.[18] I return to and evaluate this claim in the next chapter.

Rousseau

Although Enlightenment use of Cynic themes resulted in some decidedly subversive literary output, this uptake nonetheless produced a further "transvaluation" of Cynic ideas.[19] The work and life of Jean-Jacques Rousseau provides an interesting example of this process of adjustment. Rousseau was attacked for being a degenerate Cynic—"I only consider him Diogenes' dog or rather like a dog descended from a bastard of that dog" was Voltaire's assessment.[20] In Rousseau's defense, it can be argued that he only adopted the moniker in the most half-hearted, self-deprecating way: "For shyness I became a Cynic and mocker, and I pretended to scorn deeply the good manners I had been unable to acquire," he wrote.[21] Rousseau had good reason to exercise caution when self-identifying as a Cynic, since he had long been labeled and dismissed as such by others. His critics attributed to Rousseau the worst aspects of Cynicism, complaining that he was not a true citizen of the world after all, but a "misanthropic, rude, and plebeian Cynic," "an enemy not just to society … but to morality itself."[22] Somewhat complicating his image, toward the end of his life Rousseau engaged in a period of itinerant living and embarrassingly frank autobiographical writing. An unsympathetic reading would be to argue that Rousseau revealed himself in his autobiographical writings to be a bit of a half-assed Cynic, and an isolated and pathetic one at that.[23] A more favorable reading understands what his contemporaries took to be the "madness" of his last years of odd lodging and unhinged writing as constituting a Cynic pursuit of poverty and parrhesia to the point of scandal.[24]

Whatever Rousseau's intentions in those last years, and however he pictured the extent and nature of his Cynicism, if we consider his work as a whole its association with Cynicism by detractors and supporters alike is understandable. It has been argued that Rousseau "pursues an essentially Diogenical critique of civilization," though he does not always package it as such.[25] Most notably Cynic is Rousseau's attack on the sciences, arts, and polite society more generally for dressing itself up in finery amid widespread corruption. His contemporaries achieved only the semblance of virtue, Rousseau argued. Consequently, all decorum could only be judged insincere and duplicitous. Modern philosophy did not escape his contempt, with Rousseau claiming that the pursuit of reason was deforming its followers so that they were becoming egocentric, immune to the suffering of their fellow creatures, and estranged from their fellow men. On this point Rousseau criticized philosophers such as Thomas Hobbes and Bernard Mandeville for claiming that self-interest was the ultimate motive of human action.[26] This is significant, since we find Rousseau attacking what some might see as one of the basic claims of modern cynicism, which holds out little hope for humanity given its assumption that all human behavior is basically selfish. Though "cynics" of this sort are blamed for their corrosive effects on institutional life, for being a drain on the polity, and for betraying the very ideals of justice, fraternity, and reason that we inherit from the Enlightenment, Rousseau, for his part, lays the blame squarely at the door of reason and philosophy. This unpardonable suggestion, which Sloterdijk takes up and runs with two centuries later, makes modern cynicism a product of Enlightenment reason, as much as it is its opponent.[27] Modern conservatives (who follow Hobbes, not Rousseau) clearly locate the rot elsewhere. The very egocentric attitudes that Rousseau attributed to civilization are essentialized as natural to human beings. As Sloterdijk argues, this was the attitude of those conservatives who greeted the failure of the French Revolution with "horrified satisfaction," and greet it still as confirmation that human nature, set loose, "deserves no optimism." "Nothing since then," Sloterdijk adds, "has nourished the conservative image of humanity more strongly." "Without first asking about contexts," it decides that human beings behave egotistically, and greedily, and uses this low view of humanity to justify its disciplinary, authoritarian tendencies.[28]

In further provocation to his contemporaries, Rousseau claimed that historical progress was an illusion, a product of his era's delusions of preeminence. Having reconceived civilization as "a wasteland of empty social forms and behaviours,"[29] Rousseau was led to the conclusion that only by returning to the presocial state of nature is it possible to "wipe away the accretions to the human personality added since the advent of civilization."[30] It is at this point, perhaps, in his appeal to nature as a grounding principle, that Rousseau departs most obviously from ancient Cynicism. As argued in chapters 2 and 3, Diogenes appealed to natural, mainly bodily functions, as part of a wider, improvised critique of hubris and refinement. To the extent that Diogenes taught via a "return to nature," this was a tactical move, designed to scandalize society with the very disavowals on which it is built. Hence ancient Cynicism managed to put forward a critique of society without positing nature as a philosophical concept or normative ideal.

Unlike Cynic teaching, Rousseau's contrasting, normative appeal to nature has been widely appreciated and set to work as an educational philosophy, having a significant and fairly immediate impact on educational thought and practice via his 1762 treatise, *Émile, or On Education*.[31] Though Rousseau was attacked for abandoning his own offspring to a foundling hospital, his thought on education burdened all subsequent children with bourgeois hopes for "another world." As Sloterdijk argues, unlike aristocratic hopes and ambitions, which are directed at lineage (and in relation to which the child draws secondary significance), bourgeois ambition is attached directly to the child, with parental love and personal investment forming a sometimes-pernicious amalgam.[32] As a mainstay of subsequent progressive thought, *Émile* helped frame what I call the cynicism of modern progressive educators and their love of education (which is an entirely different type of cynicism from that of modern conservatives just mentioned). Just like the liberal, academic cynicism discussed above, this cynicism is again hard to draw out because of its insistent positivity. It is associated with those who assume that education is underpinned by, and can return to, an essential goodness, where the practical challenge is one of removing the worst artifices of technological civilization that imprint on and unduly restrain the free development of the child. The claimed effects of this healing of education will not simply be an improvement in the experience of children, but will be felt at a political level too, where better, more progressive education leads to a better and more harmonious society. Amid such educational hopes, which even in their most jaded form still rely on a basic refusal to entertain doubt about the mission of education, the cynicism of educationalists, of those who still believe in education, is deep set. This insistence on principle (implied if not stated) that education is, at core, naturally good once it is freed from the shackles of didactic teaching and paternalism, is the origin of the positive (but duplicitous) cynicism of educators who respond to the traumas of modernity by perpetuating a

Insistence that education is naturally good once it is freed from the shackles of didactic teaching and paternalism is the origin of the positive (but duplicitous) cynicism of educators who perpetuate a myth of educational redemption.

myth of educational redemption. The problem is this: to the extent that such educators do not entirely abandon the figure of the teacher and the necessity of some kind of educational artifice, they must remain attached to some form of disciplinary control. In a situation of this sort, as the educator seeks to free the pupil from the imprisoning effects of "bad education," he or she will celebrate just how much discrimination is exercised in the exertion of his or her educational "good will."[33] The dissembling character of Rousseau, this "master of an artful reflexivity that skilfully found fault with others on every point but in itself always discovered only the purest of intentions,"[34] sits very much at the inception of these ideas.

Diderot

A further transvaluation of Cynicism occurs in *Rameau's Nephew*,[35] an imaginary dialogue between a philosopher *Moi* (Me) and his nephew *Lui* (Him), written by Denis Diderot, who was among other things editor of the famous *Encyclopédie*. It was composed during his "underground years" following the *Encyclopédie*'s suppression in 1759, and is thought to be a product, in part, of Diderot's growing disillusionment and bitterness.[36] Perhaps as a consequence, in *Rameau's Nephew* both C/cynicisms appear to be at work. Though the nephew depicted in the conversation makes mischief by unmasking "the pretenses and the corruption of the mid-eighteenth-century Parisian literati," and in that respect performs his role as Cynic to good effect, he nonetheless accepts that social context as a "fait accompli" and "accommodates himself to reality as best he can ... in the name of survival and profit."[37] This has been described as a two-step move—the defining move of modern cynicism—where "we move from the first, incomplete step of cynicism, a depiction of a false, hypocritical society, to its second, crucial component, a tactical wager that one stands to profit more from complicity than moral purity."[38] Clearly absent here is the Cynic drive to overthrow the social order that such hypocrisies reveal. This drive is replaced by a mode of critique which acknowledges that it must be as contemptible as those it impugns (a mode of critique that had its precursors, as discussed in the previous chapter). What distinguishes the nephew in this respect is his explicitly stated "self-conscious complicity in the very culture he exposes as irredeemably corrupt."[39] The nephew is not enraged by his inescapable complicity; he does not rail against it. Rather, he welcomes and affirms it. Indeed, the nephew rebukes himself for "*failing to be complicit enough* in a society composed of lying, betraying flatterers."[40] Hence, the Cynic's free and courageous speech becomes in Rameau's nephew mere impudence, a form of entertainment. The amusement and jesting that the nephew provides is, moreover, of a highly restricted sort. Though Rameau's nephew "stirs people up and gives them a shaking," as Diderot narrates, he'd nonetheless "wormed his way into several good homes ... on condition that he did not speak unless permission had been given."[41] The Cynic's appeal to a life lived according to nature (designed to cast light on the pretensions of civilized existence) is repeated in Rameau, but nature is now redefined as a battle for survival, recommending self-interested compliance with the corrupted norms of one's social habitat. Here, the Cynic mantra "Deface the currency" is enacted not to overthrow the norms governing one's existence but to attack the ideals foisted on one's existence by a small group of philosophers. It is argued that the nephew offers a "perverse parody" of Enlightenment philosophy in this respect, by adopting its commitment to a "secular, materialist vision of humanity," and by refusing entirely to "accord any transcendent status or dignified purpose to man's existence."[42] The nephew takes that thought to its endpoint, to the most reductive materialism, when he declares: "The most important thing is to evacuate the bowels easily, freely, pleasantly, and copiously every evening. *O stercus pretiosum!* [Oh precious dung!] That is the final outcome of life in every sphere."[43] Deciding that everything is shit, yet finding pleasure in the art of shitting, the nephew's Cynicism ends up justifying his attachment to the status quo. It is worth noting, however, that Rameau's nephew has not yet retreated to the jaded, shy cynicism that Sloterdijk detects. He is not a cynic in the late modern sense. Unlike his late modern descendants, he is open about his complicity, and as a critic still has the energy and appetite for combative, prolonged confrontations.

Sade

It is claimed that the Marquis de Sade—a French noble-man and philosopher famous for his libertine writing and personal exploits—effects yet another transvaluation of Cynicism by transforming the "frank Cynic" into the "master of hypocrisy."[44] This can be seen in the character Dolmancé, the arch-libertine of Sade's 1795 *Philosophy in the Bedroom*.[45] Acting as an educator in amorality and libertinage, Dolmancé helps the fifteen-year old Eugéne "see through the veneer of our moral codes."[46] Morality, compassion, and modesty are ridiculous notions to be jet-tisoned, Dolmancé explains, since they impede the pursuit of pleasure. As I have remarked elsewhere, Sade's writings are educational—indeed they are relentlessly, tediously so.[47] They are instructional too. *Philosophy in the Bedroom* begins with an address "To Libertines," in which the reader is similarly invited to engage with the book as a tutee. We are to "study the cynical Dolmancé," Sade writes, so as to "proceed like him." We are to travel as far as our lechery takes us, "exploring and enlarging the sphere of [our] tastes and whims," sacrificing everything to the senses.[48] Sade's lesson is not one of total, unrestrained indulgence, however, at least not at first, and this is where Dolmancé becomes a master of hypocrisy. Dolmancé teaches his pupil the necessity of a little dissimulation. He encourages Eugéne to rebel against conventional mores while instructing her in the operations of deceit and subterfuge so that she may keep her libertinage hidden. This was after all a philosophy of the bedroom, not the street.

Elsewhere in his corpus Sade's libertines do travel beyond the bedroom.[49] Here Sade's cynicism appears as if it were a parody of its ancestor, where the Cynic injunction to live in accordance with nature (designed in part to free the Cynic from the moral force of shame) becomes for the libertine a social norm that "makes free sex an obligation, not an option."[50] This injunction to "enjoy" one another and ourselves, to explore all permutations of pleasure and experience without restraint, provides the underpinning logic of Sade's work, in which Sade's libertines investigate all conceivable permutations of bodily sensation to the expense of those involved. As I explore in the final chapter, this injunction to maximize enjoyment is a repressive function that underpins modern cynicism. It, too, ties pleasure to destruction, though its operations are far better cloaked.

Sade does not only offer a way into the critique of modern cynicism, however. Nor does he simply contort Cynic philosophy (which, one might object, was not governed by the pursuit of pleasure, even though it has long been dismissed for being, at core, a pleasure-seeking philosophy).[51] Sade's work extends a recognizably Cynic project to the Enlightenment, subverting Western cultural frameworks by amplifying them, revealing their grotesque nature so that they become available to criticism. To anticipate a term that will recur in the following chapter, Sade's most accomplished libertines realize their nihilism. They follow through with the tradition of Western metaphysics that associates being with a higher realm, denigrating the world below for its being mired in processes of transient becoming. Enlightenment materialism never overcame the hangover that this intoxicated point of view produced, where the world below, our world, is still nothing by comparison to the world above, a cultural prejudice that Sade takes great pleasure in exploiting. He pushes this "disavowal of reality" (and of women in particular) on which "the language of the West" was built to its limits,[52] by treating its members as they conceptualize themselves: as worth nothing, or more gently put, as having no independent worth in the absence of metaphysical standards of judgment.

Sade subverts education in a similar way by exaggerating its attempts to master the self and others.[53] Though the Western drive to mastery has been assailed for the colonial violence and environmental disaster it entails, critiques of the complicity of intellectual mastery in that violence are less common and more delicately framed.[54] With Sade, by contrast, intellectual mastery takes prominence as the root form and underpinning drive behind the violence he

Sade's work extends a recognizably Cynic project to the Enlightenment, subverting Western cultural frameworks by amplifying them, revealing their grotesque nature so that they become available to criticism.

depicts. The Socratic pedigree of intellectual aggression is indicated by Sade's use of the term *socratiser* ("to socratize") to describe the act of sticking a finger in the anus. This is not simply an erotic act, but an examination. It has been argued that one of Sade's major contributions to pedagogic technique is to accompany the traditional oral examination with an anal one, as a reminder, perhaps, of the ancient Greek link between pedagogy and pederasty.[55] The libertine will enter the body by any means, cutting into it if necessary to investigate and draw out its innards (and what, after all, does education attempt, as it studies children, seeking to draw out from what is already there?). Cool and rational, the intellect affirms itself as an active participant in the horror. The horror it perpetuates is indeed integral to the self-development of that presiding intellect. As Simone de Beauvoir observed, the Sadean libertine never "loses himself in his animal nature"; his perversions are so premeditated and cerebral that "philosophic discourse, far from dampening his ardour, acts as an aphrodisiac."[56] With Sade, we find the wildest hopes of philosophy and education realized; "a lucid mind inhabits a body which is being degraded into matter."[57] In this scheme, self-mastery does not take the conventional form of self-abasement, chastisement, and bodily restraint. Instead, it is devastatingly affirmative. Libertine self-mastery is realized in attempts to overcome all conventions, norms, and restrictions, including the operations of a conscience, which prevent the libertine from pursuing his or her will to power without check. The body is overcome by excess, not restraint. This is, nonetheless, a disciplinary excess.[58] Indeed, if we view the long tradition of self-mastery not as a system of repression but as a technology of the self that constitutes us in its attempts to educate the body and form its being, libertine self-mastery can be seen as an exaggeration, not a reversal. Sade merely lifts the lid on that activity as the libertine attempts to exhaust all possible contortions of bodily existence. Libertine mastery exceeds everything that holds investigation back, allowing the libertine intellect to pursue all permutations of horror with calculative zeal—anticipating, perhaps, the integration of intellectual work within the destructive impulse of modern technocratic rationality.

In Sade's writing, we find the drive to sovereign mastery that underpins Western education and philosophy pushed to its abysmal conclusion: the destruction of Humankind, God, and Nature.[59] By implication, if anything is to be retained of ancient Cynicism as a militant philosophy, it must develop beyond the self-defeating, world-denying consequences of a drive to mastery, beyond the mastery (and destruction) of others and their environment. Although ancient Cynic mastery might be contrasted with other forms of sovereign composure that seek to regulate and form the body in the name of a higher calling (this being the formula that governs Western education), and although it might be defended as promoting a strain of mastery that affirms rather than denies experience, as Sade makes clear, mastery can still be destructive (and not in a generative way), even at its most wildly affirmative. This is not to argue that mastery in either form should be simply rejected. As a salutary note, this is the endpoint the libertine reaches in Sade's writing, where the libertine discovers that his or her last remaining bind is to the quest for mastery itself. Its abandonment leaves the libertine romping without purpose, ceaselessly active—aimlessly so, in ways that seem to anticipate a direction of travel that today's educator may begin to recognize.[60]

LIVE THE END TIMES: THE MANY FACES OF MODERN CYNICS

There is no space here to chart the subsequent development of modern cynicism through the nineteenth and twentieth centuries, though it is worth indicating where such an account might begin. Building on previous work, we might start with the modification of cynicism by the Counter-Enlightenment.[1] Representatives of that movement, such as Edmund Burke, along with contemporaries of his who were participating in a wider propaganda war against the French Revolution that was bankrolled by the British government, worked together in attacking and travestying the Cynic Rousseau. Though his attackers would not have pictured themselves in this way, as they submitted Rousseau to a thorough chewing over, they participated in the further development of modern cynicism. Burke famously argued against the kinds of abstract intellectualism he associated with the Enlightenment in favor of a more practical, pragmatic accommodation to the everyday forces of unthinking prejudice and tradition. Historically accrued conventions and habits should be valued for their social usefulness and contribution to stability rather than demolished, Burke claimed. In making this argument, Burke reinstated the very forces that the Enlightenment had sought to overcome. Given that, in Burke's view, the uneducated masses are unaware of the (socially conservative) value to existing society of their unthinking conventions and habits, men such as himself should be tasked with identifying and defending these British "virtues," ensuring they remain undisturbed by any kind of revolutionary agitation. British habits and their accompanying institutions and hierarchies are said to require the gentle guidance of liberal gentlemen of a Burkean persuasion, and should be protected from any kind of radical or hasty adjustment. Though Burke would certainly not adopt the term "cynic," he nonetheless displayed what one might describe as a uniquely modern, paternalistic form of cynicism, a form of cynicism that underpins the logic of government manipulation and institutional care. It is the cynicism of those who seek to shape public opinion by manipulating its already existing tendencies and habits. This is the cynicism of spin doctors, media empires, social networking sites, data analysts, politicians, PR firms, image consultants, advertising agencies, and lifestyle coaches. Such agencies clearly further their own interests as well as the interests of power and capital, and in that sense follow a narrow dictionary definition of cynicism. But this is not all they do. Their cynic paternalism takes a more developed form as these activities are understood and justified, namely, as activities that will also benefit those they manipulate, either by serving "the public" configured as a social and political abstraction, or by diverting it with an endless array of life hacks, memes, and consumer goods. This very claim—to assist the public it exploits, to help a public it will never trust to help itself—is at the root of its cynicism.

The Critique of Cynicism

Typical depictions of modern cynicism do not focus on its paternalistic or beneficent side. In the popular imagination modern cynicism is portrayed very differently, as an individual flaw, or a social malaise, that requires urgent attention if not remedial action. According to its detractors, it is characterized by suspicion of higher ideals and a retreat from the public realm to a private sphere of stoked up, injurious grievances. This retreat is associated with a dismissal of the positive value of critique, a distrust of collective solutions and institutional interventions, a refusal to invest any hope in social and political reform, and a selective deafness directed toward all calls to social action and transformation, which are rejected outright and in advance for their futility.[2]

When civil society and its social institutions are blamed for their role in producing cynical attitudes, they are only gently impugned for giving populations undue reason to be cynical, as a result of occasional lapses in good governance, as an effect of various flaws and failures, scandals, and shenanigans that have been made public by the occasional whistle-blower and the operations of a zealous press. The great stupidity of mass cynicism, from this point of view, lies with its inability to distinguish between good and bad governance. Mass cynicism is an irrational, exaggerated state of disappointment, a near infantile mode of response to individual cases of inadequacy, institutional failure, or corruption. Having reacted disproportionately, contemporary cynics cut themselves off, transforming disappointment into a cynic determination to disregard all offices and institutions as inevitably flawed. Deciding that nothing can be done, or that all effort will eventually come to naught, the cynic abdicates individual responsibility, commits to political indifference, and contributes thereby to the further erosion of everything the cynic bemoans.

The solution envisaged in this critique of cynicism is to restore the institutions of democratic society so that they may once again adequately serve, provide, and care for their citizenry, clawing back due respect that was lost in many cases undeservedly, or at least too absolutely, restoring faith, healing communities, returning meaning and purpose to social and political life, and reconstructing the public realm on which that meaning depends. The path of restoration is arduous and long, but the stakes are too high to abandon it. Modern cynicism is approached as a personal and interpersonal epidemic that requires extended treatment. This restorative process must be patronized and resourced adequately if it is to succeed, which demands among other things the very existence, intellectual fortitude, expenditure of time, resources, and goodwill of the educated critic and writer of books against cynicism. These books may express their own disappointment, but the discontent of the educated critic (in contrast to the infantile, excessive disappointment of the contemporary cynic) is measured and targeted. Dismayed by a populace that does not think in their image, critics bemoan those who do not respond with collective outrage, those who have yet to mobilize against the forces of injustice that the social critic describes with such righteous indignation. Collective apathy is the typical diagnosis; it is a consequence of their cynicism. Its critics decide that what cynicism demands is more of the same, that is to say, more of them, as they offer further critical insights, careful diagnoses, visionary mission statements, reasons to listen, and declarations of optimism. Critics discover that the problem with contemporary cynics is that they lack a political imagination. Commentators identify an intellectual, imaginative deficit permeating mainstream culture to which they respond with offerings of their own. This cynicism, they argue, has become a routine, banal mode of interaction, a habitual point of view and way of seeing the world that automates contempt and manufactures distrust, and thereby continues to operate as a self-reinforcing prophecy of its own continued existence. As a social ill, it requires among other things an injection of hope to rescue its sufferers from their unwarranted negativity, which saps people's confidence in politics and public officials who, so the cynic wrongly, too absolutely assumes, are driven by a will to power, and as such, forgo their commitment to the public good in favor of personal advancement. This jaded cynicism interprets all actions, however apparently noble, as driven by base inclinations. From the cynic point of view, democratically elected politicians are more concerned with winning than governing, professionals are more concerned with career advancement, and companies more concerned with profit and protection against litigation, than they are with public service. All these assumptions must be countered.

This cynicism is said to be the product of a dangerous, self-denying, socially destructive lack of faith, a dogmatic, unthinking rejection of all efforts to social betterment. It is the condition of those who operate on the blanket assumption that individuals and institutions are driven before all else by a self-serving impulse, an inbuilt and insatiable greed, and therefore cannot be trusted. Those who rail against the malignant effects of this cynical condition complain that cynics are guilty of extending their own reduced understanding of the world to others. From this point of view, the psychological and sociological realism of the cynic, the cynic's claim to have seen to the bottom of things, is really nothing but an expression of the cynic's own abject selfishness and moral impoverishment. Suffering in this way, cynics overgeneralize their own diminished outlook and extend it to those who have not yet lost all hope in human possibility. Modern cynicism, this complaint continues, is the regrettably widespread condition of those who assume that everyone else is as cynical as they are, a baseline assumption that seals the cynic within his or her own self-reinforcing assumptions about the state of the world. Pictured in this way, contemporary cynicism is held responsible for a multitude of ills ranging from disaffection, political apathy, and cultural decline, to a dangerous lack of faith in Enlightenment ideals and the internal weakening of liberal democracies. As a cultural phenomenon it is blamed for a general lack of commitment to the institutions and cultural values of those polities, as well as the kind of blanket skepticism and suspicion of truth-claims, expertise, and authority that give rise to the phenomenon of "post-truth" politics.[3]

Though individual critiques—including many of those cited above and below—may set out their stall with care, they nonetheless support or at least play into a pejorative use of the term "cynic" that is typified by its attachment to others, always others. The word "cynic" is mobilized, without irony, to express disappointment at *other* people's disappointment at the state of things. This cynicism, so targeted, is blamed for its politically deleterious effects, including: a lack of commitment to shared endeavors or community initiatives that must themselves be under-pinned by a commitment to the common good; a tendency to give up far too soon in the face of adversity; and a selfish determination to survive circumstance but offer nothing back—in sum, for a collection of ills that must inevitably lead to political and social disaster.

Though there is much worth attending to in this list of grievances, the overall framing of this critique of cynicism is nonetheless problematic. To continue the ar-gument made earlier, one might suggest that those who complain about and write against cynicism in this way of-fer fitting examples of its disavowed paternalistic under-side. All these complaints against cynicism function as so many justifications for the moral seriousness and social necessity of the person who draws attention to the danger of cynicism. They are based on a suspicion of a populace that cannot be trusted to govern itself without the expert, moral intervention of the social critic, academic special-ist, media columnist, welfare professional, and political careerist, together with the institutional forces he or she

Those who complain
about and write
against cynicism
offer fitting examples
of its disavowed
paternalistic underside.

represents. The attraction and self-affirming satisfaction to be found in a critique of contemporary cynicism is such that in recent years the popular and academic presses have been flooded with complaints against cynicism, ranging from its apparent destruction of the American Dream[4] to its erosive effects on interpersonal relationships.[5] It is the bogey, or great evil, that confronts journalists with indifference,[6] saps hope and authenticity from education,[7] facilitates criminal warmongering and disregard of international rule of law,[8] tears apart families and communities, and denies us a better future. A tendency to rail against cynicism can, in short, serve to distract us from the co-implication of the institutions it is said to undermine, in its very production.

Radical Left Grievances

To gather up a further selection of grievances, focusing now more exclusively on radical left rather than progressive, liberal humanist, and conservative responses, it is notable that, although the political stakes are adjusted, modern cynicism is again blamed for its politically anesthetizing effects. Mass cynicism has been condemned for pervading the multitude (the collective exploited by capitalism) with "bad sentiments," rendering it more susceptible to capitalism's whims.[9] This cynicism is not conceptualized as a personal flaw—or not only—but is systematically produced by capital. It is understood to be the more or less direct product of late capitalist exploitation, of a system that is built, according one recent characterization, on the "intimate diffusion and viral corruption of life by capital, deleting its potential and recoding it into a subject and agent of productive behaviours."[10] Individuals become alienated from themselves, unable to find purchase within a system of power that has itself become extremely diffuse, that pervades daily life, that manifests everywhere as an insidious presence that has all but colonized us as human beings. With power no longer (just) centralized in dominant institutions but distributed "through vast networks of information and finance," with power no longer easily identifiable or assailable, a population will almost inevitably fall into a state of collective fatalism, despair, and apathy if the causes of its cynicism are not grasped and countered by a mass mobilization, by activities that prove to a populace that it does still have within its grasp the means to change its future and combat the co-option of life by capital through noncynical, hopeful, collective action.[11] The stakes could not be higher, because, according to the severest possible assessment, the "sardonic laughter" of today's cynic may ultimately be in league with fascism.[12] The sheer scope of modern cynicism is part of the problem. It is said to range from "ignorant indifference or disaffected disappointment to an informed callousness," with little or nothing of positive note in between.[13] From this perspective, as a product of structural forces, mass cynicism can perhaps be forgiven for its "stupidity" so long as it yields to remedy.

Less forgivable, for some, are the fashionable cynicisms of "left" postmodern theory, which are blamed for inviting skepticism before all truth claims, and doubt before our ability to submit the world about us to the dictates, and progressive impulses of reason. In this context, "cynicism" becomes a synonym for postmodernism, construed as "a debased cultural form, a monstrous hybrid aesthetic, a decadent self-indulgent apoliticism and an élitist, ironical nihilism."[14] Postmodernism is here characterized as fundamentally cynical, though "not cynically *suffering*, like Sloterdijk's melancholic victim of enlightenment, but cynically *destructive*, the perpetrator of a sinister assault on cognitive, aesthetic and moral certainties."[15] I would argue that those railing against this specific type of "cynicism" tend to misunderstand its nature, misread its intent, and then vastly overestimate its reach and influence. And yet, such critics of "postmodern" theory will find a sympathetic audience. This accusation of "cynicism" is one way in which hegemonic (and apparently counter-hegemonic) thought gives itself permission to dismiss what it cannot assimilate. These so-called intellectual cynicisms—often most closely associated with French postwar philosophy—are then rejected as the product of failed and disappointed "revolutionaries" who spent their remaining years justifying to themselves why they gave up on radical collective action. The French cultural theorist Jean Baudrillard—renowned for his work on our apparent inability to distinguish reality from its simulation—is given as the typical example of the "catatonic" effects of cynical "left" theory.[16] Michel Foucault, to give another example, has also been taken to task for adopting the "cynical gaze of the genealogist."[17] But individual examples will not suffice to get a full measure of the "creep" of postmodern ideas into the academy, we are told. Its critics hope that this is a "temporary, reactionary 'blip' of irrationality in the greater dialectical movement of History." We might look back on this period one day as a time when academics colonized the space opened by their postmodern doubt "by theorizing it so exhaustively," a time that suffered from an "essentially momentary failure of rational and political nerve," a failure, a retreat that would soon be overcome by a "heroic" return to politics, understood and embraced as an essentially antagonistic endeavor, one that requires "bravado and virtuosity," not excuses for inaction.[18]

Radical left grievances against cynicism, then, are just as damning as their conservative and liberal equivalents. Across the board, and despite important differences in perspective, there is broad consensus that a crisis of the political needs to be challenged by promoting new forms of democratic sociality and political engagement. As a result of its prior condemnation, the possible role of modern cynicism in that political undertaking is ruled out. Yet modern cynicism is not just a feature of capitalist society,[19] nor is it simply the product of a crisis in democratic sociality.[20] As several recent studies of its history have pointed out, contemporary cynicism has been in gestation for some considerable time.[21]

Late Soviet Cynicism

For one notable departure from the blanket assumption that cynicism has no positive role to play in social transformation, it is worth turning to Alexei Yurchak's study of the last Soviet generation in which he unpacks what he calls the "cynical reason of late socialism."[22] Though Soviet ideology was still experienced by this generation as "immutable and omnipresent," Yurchak claims that it was also greeted with widespread indifference.[23] The success of Soviet ideology did not stand or fall on its ability to secure the widespread support of a populace that *believed* in it, at least not in its twilight years. It was a matter of irrelevance whether one believed or not. Late Soviet ideology was not hegemonic as a result of its ability to dupe or fool its populace into accepting it as "truth." It did not function by convincing a citizenry to "buy in" to its distorted view of the world. Rather, its stability was reflected in the fact that few believed the Soviet political order would end. Here there is a parallel with the experience of contemporary Western capitalist society; its continued existence seems inevitable. Consequently, its institutional, political, and social rituals are performed even where they are not believed. There is a key difference, nonetheless: Western performativities play out across "democratic" institutional frameworks, where citizens may still "buy in" to the idea that their political participation is of some value and importance, however small. These democratic frameworks are characterized moreover by their apparent openness to and reliance on diversity; difference is rendered productive. In the Soviet context, by contrast, official discourse was undisguisedly monolithic, and with the exception of the occasional ideologue, few believed that they could meaningfully participate in it. For these reasons, it is probable that Soviet ideology was accompanied by a higher level of cynicism, one distinguished by a more complete lack of interest in power. It was expressed in the attitude of those who participated in the rituals of Soviet society without finding them at all meaningful. Hence the following recollection: "It was not uncommon to hold official signs or banners with slogans during parades without reading them and to carry a portrait of a Politburo member without knowing who exactly it was."[24] Belief and commitment were largely simulated, their hollow observance automated to such an extent that they need not come into conflict with a growing nonofficial realm of cynic derision and ironic detachment.

Yurchak argues that within this parallel existence, a uniquely cynical form of humor took hold. The obligatory reeling off and sharing of political jokes or *anekdoty* in private became commonplace. Such humor could be understood as an expression of distance, a symptom of the growing separation of cynic subjectivity from official Soviet ideology. But it can also be understood as an expression of the fact that laughter could no longer directly hurt power. Laugher, derision, and critique cannot embarrass an official order so debased it is reflexively buffered by its own falseness. Hence wit and derision were not in direct conflict with officialdom because official symbols were experienced as already false, concocted to such an extent that they barely warranted critique. Having given up all investment in the possible overthrow of the official sphere, late socialist cynicism was only quietly subversive of it. Its subversions were not self-consciously transformative in their intent, nor did they openly target power. This was a cynicism of expediency and survival. It was based in the discovery that a safe and enjoyable existence was still possible in a totalitarian society so long as the cynic took no active interest in official pronouncements. And yet, by entirely disregarding, by not even bothering to confront or give too much thought to official slogans, this cynicism contributed to the undoing of that Soviet social order. Soviet people learned "how to take part in ideological practices 'without really being there.'" As claimed by one of its own, the last Soviet generation achieved remarkably high levels of "mental non-involvement in the official sphere."[25]

It "developed sophisticated strategies for producing parallel culture right inside and in spite of the official order
without needing to worry too much about the latter." This
cynic disregard, so the argument goes, is what ultimately
led to the "inner 'silent' crisis and erosion" of the Soviet
system.[26] The cynicism of late socialism quietly preceded
and prepared the way for its spectacular collapse.

Sloterdijk's Critique

Perhaps the most useful and illuminating discussion of
modern cynicism remains Sloterdijk's *Critique of Cynical
Reason*. Sloterdijk's book provides a sustained analysis
of its "physiognomy," or surface features, explaining why
mass cynicism is so hard to dislodge. Though Sloterdijk's
critique has become a staple reference point for a small
number of "left" theorists, it rarely intrudes much further
than the obligatory footnote.[27] Here Sloterdijk is most
commonly credited for his description of mass cynicism
as "enlightened false consciousness."[28] More widely, the
book is notable for its absence from or marginal presence
within most subsequent critiques of cynicism, particularly
those of a conservative or liberal persuasion. Though it
offers probably the most sophisticated, intellectually ambitious survey of modern cynicism to date, it lacks the
kind of seriousness and rigor expected of academic work,
and perhaps as a result suffers from what has been described as the "customary academic suspicion of anything

that is not guaranteed to be mediocre."[29] The form as well as the overall argument of the book appears a little too scandalous for the majority of critics and bemoaners of cynicism to take on board, and only a tiny minority give serious attention to Sloterdijk's suggested remedy.[30] Here Sloterdijk argues for a revival of ancient Cynic *Frechheit* or effrontery, favoring the insolent or impertinent behavior of the ancient Cynic to the "reflexively buffered"[31] negativity of the modern cynic. Sloterdijk seeks to disarm a subject whose destructive force has become patently obvious: "Only at the peak of modernity does the identity of subjectivity and armament reveal itself to us," Sloterdijk claims, as that identity, that co-implication of late modern subjectivity and armament brings "the global destruction of the world into practical reach."[32] This destructive arrangement is brought into stark relief today in the form of Trump's White House tweets, though it is expressed too in the everyday micro-aggressions enacted by an essentially violent subjectivity. Cynic *Frechheit* is Sloterdijk's solution; it is the basis of a proposed transformation in subjectivity, where a revived Cynicism softens the violent, world-destroying ego in laughter.[33] The form of Sloterdijk's book very much models that argument, as it toys with respectable scholarly norms and makes mischief with its reader. As one of its more perceptive readers has pointed out, Sloterdijk's "whirlwind tour of modern Cynics leaves us out of breath, grasping for something to hold on to."

Sloterdijk's thought makes so many unlikely associations, and does so at such a pace, that the reader struggles to keep up. Which is precisely the point: "I surmise that Sloterdijk intended us to scratch our heads, bewildered, at his *satura*, or potpourri, until we burst out laughing."[34] Sloterdijk's alterity as a critic of cynicism should not be exaggerated, however. Despite Sloterdijk's impudent proposal, his critique of cynical reason falls in with all other critiques (with the exception of Yurchak's) insofar as it finds modern cynicism deplorable.

Insurrectional Potential

This book departs from the positions outlined so far that seek to lessen or overcome modern cynicism. It attends to the insurrectional potential of contemporary cynicism, exploring the idea of its *intensification*. This is something more than straightforward exaggeration: it represents an attempt to adopt, test, and transform the most banal and yet dangerous features of contemporary cynicism. I realize this may strike most readers as a reckless line of inquiry, if not deplorable in its own way. And there is good reason for caution. It remains the case that cynicism has the potential to lead a public already disenchanted and impatient with the inconclusive nature of a more engaged, "genuine" politics to "a still more conservative embrace of those who already project power and authority."[35] Contemporary cynicism is indeed a corrosive presence. And yet, modern cynicism, on the whole, is far less devastatingly critical than is often feared, tending as it does to leave untouched the "fundamental level of ideological fantasy" that structures social reality.[36] Ideology maintains its hold on the cynic in the most deceptive way; the enlightened cynic feels that he or she has become conversant in the operations of the former, and believes that this knowledge is sufficient to escape its grasp.[37] This may indeed account for the key statement of modern cynicism: "cynics know what they are doing, but still they do it."[38] Yet, cynic complicity with power is not inevitable. Occasionally, the attitude of modern cynicism is expressed with devastating force, as a morally disillusioned, politically disaffected distrust of the ideals and promises of modernity and its institutions, educational and otherwise. This kind of ferocious distrust might still be harnessed to a revolutionary politics that does not shrink from the necessity of overcoming the current order.

My approach in this discussion of modern cynicism clearly avoids a moralistic rejection of it as basically destructive of democratic sociality, where our collective affliction by cynicism is understood as ranging between an individual disorder and a cultural malaise requiring treatment. This perception, as pointed out above, frames dominant popular understandings of cynicism configured as a social problem and underpins prominent critiques of its corrosive presence. The approach adopted here also avoids attempts by liberal-minded thinkers—comparatively rare but not insignificant—to cast modern cynicism as a potentially useful critical disposition.[39] We are told that cynicism could be adopted strategically rather than absolutely, allowing democratic actors to survive an "always compromised, always impure political realm" as they strive for progressive change.[40] It can, we are assured, be "managed and mobilized" (by the good) "in ways that are perfectly hospitable to the continued, healthy functioning of democratic life."[41] In small doses, a tempered cynicism might even help defend cultures of openness and free speech, and encourage the kind of social and political vigilance that keeps democracy alive. This book does not argue for such a restrained, measured cynicism. Nor does it remain within a scholarly anatomization of modern forms of cynicism—seeking to complicate our understanding of mass cynicism, depicted now as a multifaceted rather than monolithic phenomenon—and in due academic style, reserve final judgment in the face of that complexity. Such an approach is common in academic circles, where withheld judgment itself becomes a marker of intellectual sophistication. Rather, I invite consideration of the scandalous potential of modern cynicism—considered in its "lowest," most impoverished forms—where, in the style of its ancient ancestor, the dominant traits of a disavowed but culturally entrenched phenomenon are attended to for their potential adoption and positive, tactical adaptation.

This would constitute a transformation of modern cynicism through a select metamorphosis of its more dangerous attributes, moving it beyond its current position in which cynicism serves as an excuse for political inertia and inaction before injustice, manipulation, and hypocrisy. To develop this thesis, it is necessary to return to the historical narrative, such as it has been drawn, and consider the adoption of Cynic ideas by Friedrich Nietzsche in the late nineteenth century. It is necessary to switch pace, in other words, and plow back under the critical positions outlined above.

Nietzsche, Nihilism, and Half-Assed Cynics

The theme of cynicism recurs throughout the nineteenth century, having become "a byword ... for a selfish misanthropy or ... distrust, disbelief, [and] indifference to moral norms."[42] It is perhaps unsurprising, then, that Nietzsche should pick up the idea, affirm its hostility to conventional morality, and declare: "There is altogether no prouder and at the same time more exquisite kind of book than my books—they attain here and there the highest thing that can be attained on earth, cynicism."[43] Nietzsche's invocation of and contribution to the critique of Cynicism is complex.[44] It is claimed that Nietzsche's irreverent, playful style owes much to Cynicism, which he studied closely.

Perhaps from the Cynics Nietzsche derived the lesson that a thoroughgoing critique of cultural norms need not become burdened by its own seriousness, nor must it lead to a world-denying pessimism, but could instead be tied to a "pessimism of strength,"[45] an affirmation of existence by way of doubt.[46] And perhaps it was from Cynicism in part that Nietzsche borrowed the idea that only through the most unflinching, undomesticated critique of one's surroundings might one glimpse the possibility of another life. In what follows, I focus on how Nietzsche adapts the anecdote of Diogenes and the lantern.[47] In the original anecdote from Laertius's *Lives*, Diogenes wanders around with a lantern in broad daylight, announcing, "I am looking for a man."[48] The joke is that Diogenes is surrounded by men, but will not identify a single one as representing "man." In *The Gay Science*, we encounter something resembling this story, only now the madman with a lantern shouts incessantly "I seek God! I seek God!" Those standing around treat him with derision. "Has he got lost?" they ask laughingly, to which the madman replies: "Whither is God? ... I will tell you. *We have killed him*—you and I. All of us are his murderers." Do you not smell the divine putrefaction, he continues, because Gods, too, decompose? But none of those assembled seem able or willing, nor do they realize the magnitude of what they have done.[49]

This famous passage offers a condensed critique of the "destiny of two millennia of Western history," in

Heidegger's terms.[50] It explores the ontological convulsion brought about by the eventual, if only ever partial, collapse of Western metaphysics. This derangement occurred as the Enlightenment attempted to ground reason in "man," rather than establish it by appeal to external legitimating forces. Man was, of course, nowhere to be found (some jokes never grow old). Hence, despite its claims to independence, Enlightenment attempts to more fully occupy and base its efforts within a secular realm drew from and extended the work of premodern institutions on which it was forced to rely. For example, the modern school drew from and based itself within Christian pastoral institutional logics that were able to "slip their doctrinal moorings" and migrate to a secular context.[51] The key difference, however, is one of legitimation. Though earthbound institutions such as the Christian church had long been employed to make sense of and organize their subjects' earthly existence, its representatives spoke on behalf of a higher purpose, where that purpose was divined from another realm rather than reasoned from first principles. The death of God refers to the crisis of legitimation that occurs as this framework breaks down, revealing in due course the basic inability of Western subjectivity to think outside metaphysics. How can we decide what is true, just, or meaningful, this subject asks, without external standards against which we measure our pronouncements? One might claim that the ancient Cynic set out to dispute this metaphysically enframed point of view at its very inauguration, refusing, for example, to explain the meaning of Cynic practice in relation to its telos, improvising Cynic philosophy in response to circumstance rather than grounding its philosophy in a legitimating framework. The subsequent history of this Cynic refusal of the judgmental, sense-making system of Western metaphysics nonetheless demonstrates just how difficult it is to escape, which is why the Cynic battle remains an ongoing struggle to bring to existence another life against the accruements of Western civilization that would subsume and co-opt Cynic practice to its ends. Given the extent to which Cynicism was variously co-opted during more than two millennia of adjustment and transvaluation, it is unsurprising that its Enlightenment inheritors (those who attempted to free themselves from "self-incurred tutelage"[52]) found themselves entirely unprepared to deal with the collapse of the system of legitimation that ancient Cynicism once contested. Even avowed atheists, Nietzsche argues, have not come to terms with the loss of a higher, divine authority. Perhaps only contemporary cynics, of the most flippantly apathetic, casually skeptical sort, come close. Most cannot understand their existence without appeal to some external framework or other. Substitutes and stand-ins are always presumed, though it remains the case that no single candidate can occupy the position of "shared source of meaning and value," as Nietzsche might put it. "Our form of life has changed in such a way that we are no longer able to submit ourselves to such a God."[53] Instead, we late moderns switch listlessly between substitutes—reason, liberty, utility, and so on—unable to secure consensus, or, even worse, pay lip service to institutional "mission statements" that are so vapid and gestural in their construction that they do not stand up to inspection. This restless condition, Nietzsche argues, constitutes our nihilism. A nihilist, as he puts it, is one who "judges of the world as it is that it ought *not* to be, and of the world as it ought to be that it does not exist."[54] Nihilism, in this context, describes a form of dissatisfaction that we will struggle to escape. It is the condition of those who complain but lack the means to remedy their situation. It is a culturally produced disorder that afflicts the most hopeful "idealist" just as it conditions the most dejected cynic—indeed, it connects one to the other.

Here, perhaps, Nietzsche's critique of nihilism affords one of the most useful explanatory frameworks for understanding contemporary cynicism as a necessary cultural phenomenon, one that has been in gestation since the advent of Western subjectivity. As such, it can be appreciated and understood as a conflicted, melancholic state that will not accommodate itself to, or even acknowledge the consequences of, the "death of God," of a shift to modern forms of legitimation that have given up a cosmic sense of reason—a sense of our place within an order of existence that exceeds us. To quote Nietzsche once more: "This tremendous event is still on its way, it has not yet reached the ears of men"—we have not yet realized the full extent of the ontological convulsion that was brought about by the switch to modern understandings of our place within the universe.[55] Modern cynicism is what reigns in the dubious interregnum. It is the product of a failure to come to terms with loss, a failure to realize that something has been lost, or, if the loss is acknowledged, a failure to understand precisely *what* was lost in the lost object. It can be understood, by analogy, as a condition of arrested mourning—a melancholic state—to invoke Freud.[56] Understood as a failure to mourn successfully—where to properly mourn a lost object one must confront the trauma of its loss—melancholia keeps the cynic trapped. In this arrested, suffering state, "the existence of the lost object is psychically prolonged" though its presence is not easily detected.[57] It is prolonged as a disavowed attachment to things that the cynic claims to no longer believe. This melancholic condition endures with such force, and is so difficult to combat, because it is impossible to fully reconcile oneself to a loss that one can only vaguely comprehend. Suffering in this manner, modern cynicism remains stuck within an abstract but utterly debilitating sense of disappointment, the root cause of which it cannot identify or move beyond.[58] This condition of disappointment is nonetheless something one might work with, come to understand, and seek to develop, so as to help cynicism escape its melancholic entrapment and confront the underpinning trauma to which it is, as yet, an inadequate response.[59]

Like cynicism, as a descriptive term, "nihilism" is used mainly in the pejorative sense. Indeed, both have been lumped together: "Akin to nihilism, cynicism leads individuals and nations to abandon all moral values and to drown in a fetid sea of intellectual and ethical moroseness."[60] Like cynicism, nihilism requires a degree of rehabilitation as a concept before it can be meaningfully confronted. Typically, it is associated with the belief that life is meaningless and nothing is true. As such, nihilism is figured as a dangerous affliction, erosive of the social order, gratifying nothing but its own diminished outlook. But this depiction of nihilism is too absolute and dismissive, reducing a highly complex crisis in legitimation to an irrational condition of determined negativity. Conceptions such as these must be cleared away in order to reach a better understanding of how nihilism manifests in everyday behavior.

Nihilism is not entirely mired in or constituted by negativity. To take the example of education, almost nobody working within educational settings is a nihilist in the colloquial sense, since this would mean giving up entirely on the idea that education serves a purpose of some sort, whether moral or liberatory, or even just instrumental and pragmatic. To function in an educational environment it is necessary to retain some semblance of belief in education, however that idea is configured. Though educational institutions are places that nurture various forms of negativity—ranging from the systemic production of failing students, to complaints slung back and forth between staff, students, administrators, and managers, who exist uneasily alongside one another in an environment where the ultimate purpose and organizing principles of education remain unclear—all such lamentations are based on the prior condition they do not disturb the idea that education is both important and necessary. Negativity runs amok in such places, but it is not absolute, nor is it catastrophic to the idea of education. Negative sentiments can be indulged without threatening the underpinning commitment of educational spaces to the idea that they can always be improved by being rendered more educational. Every complaint against education only defers the problem of education, where more, better education is the only conceivable solution to each failure of education to deliver. Modern education is nihilistic, then, though not in the conventional sense of giving up because "nothing matters." Its nihilism resides in the demand that education must be redeemed, though by design it never can or will be. To quote Nietzsche, those who suffer education in its current forms are "sustained by a hope which cannot be refuted by any actuality—which is not *done away with* by any fulfilment: a hope in the Beyond."[61] For education, this "Beyond" takes many forms, as educational promises of fulfillment, enlightenment, and justice that are maintained, assumed, and reasserted, but never realized. This is its nihilism. It is also the cause of its cynicism, which appears in consequence of the educator's indefatigable attempts to redeem education, attempts that must fail again and again. The failing student—produced by a system that requires failure in order to conceptualize success—provides endless resource for cynicism of an unproductive, closed, and unreflective form. This cynicism takes root in the very educators or practical "idealists" who produced it by way of their "uncynical" commitment to betterment by way of education.

Education retreats from a more complete realization of its nihilism, from recognizing the nihilism of its educational optimism, though it may be better served if it embraced it. It has been argued indeed that the advent of Western nihilism is not to be regretted. While suffering it, so the argument goes, we might gain access to "the process of becoming of the 'false' constructs of metaphysics, morality, religion and art." When embraced, nihilism brings into view "the entire tissue of erring that alone constitutes the wealth or, more simply put, the essence of reality."[62] This is hardly consoling. But why must it be? Perhaps here the closely associated attitude of modern cynicism might be of some assistance, reducing our need of and desire for redemption. A more deliberate cynicism might cause us to falter in our habitual retreat to the hoped-for security of revived metaphysical frameworks and authentic political engagements. It might help resist the false promises of hope—the assurance that we might overcome our nihilism by force of will, as if it could simply be rejected. The modern cynic would achieve all this by way of a mode of critique that is just as damning for the cynic as it is for anyone else. This is what Nietzsche admired in the so-called cynics of his day, namely, "people who recognize the animal, the baseness, the 'rule' in itself, and yet still have that degree of intelligence and gumption that forces them to talk about themselves and people like them *in front of witnesses*." Occasionally, he adds, "they even wallow in books as in their own dirt," demonstrating that this much-fetishized medium offers no escape.[63]

Sloterdijk and the Code of Shitting

Sloterdijk famously introduces his critique of modern cynical reason by declaring the near death of philosophy:

> For a century now philosophy has been lying on its deathbed. ... We are enlightened, we are apathetic. No one talks any more of a *love* of wisdom. There is no longer any knowledge whose friend (*philos*) one could be.[64]

Where philosophy "has not foundered on the mere administration of thoughts, it plods on in glittering agony," haunted by the great themes and hopes it never realized.[65] Sloterdijk's outlook for education is similarly bleak, perhaps more so, given that he detects "in the air: the end of the belief in education," no less.[66] Perhaps Sloterdijk can smell better than most, but I do not sense it.[67] He writes of a growing realization that was "a certainty" in ancient Cynicism, namely the idea "that things must first be better before you can learn anything sensible."[68] This idea would indeed sound the knell of education, as we know it, though the opposite remains the case, namely, the dominant perception that learning must prefigure or drive improvement.[69] Since Sloterdijk offered his diagnosis, governments have insisted on the point: learning is no longer optional; all members of society must embrace a path of lifelong learning as if that were the route to general economic prosperity.[70] Though Sloterdijk may be right, insofar as talk of the love of wisdom and of the preeminent importance of the educated now smacks of credulity, he perhaps overstates the case. Philosophers and educators still labor away, believing, if only dimly, that what they do is oriented to improvement and betterment. Modern cynicism is driven not by generalized apathy but by *incomplete* disenchantment.

Another example of overstatement in Sloterdijk's analysis is this claim: "Because everything has become

Modern cynicism is driven not by generalized apathy but by *incomplete* disenchantment.

problematic, everything is also now a matter of indifference."[71] But modern cynics are not entirely indifferent, I would argue. They are characterized more often by a hollow cheerfulness than abject gloom. By comparison, Sloterdijk's description of present-day cynics as "borderline melancholics" is more instructive, though Sloterdijk gives too much credit to those who, he claims, maintain their existence at the border of melancholia without falling into a full-blown melancholic stupor. Sloterdijk suggests that present-day cynics survive only to the extent they "can keep their symptoms of depression under control."[72] Another interpretation of this melancholic condition, to continue the argument presented above, would be to say that present-day cynics are borderline melancholics because they have not yet entirely submitted themselves to cynicism, just as those who suffer most from the effects of nihilism, in Nietzsche's sense, have not yet come to terms with their predicament. They remain "more or less able to work,"[73] not because they keep an otherwise raging cynicism under control, but because it has not yet made its presence fully felt.

Elsewhere Sloterdijk describes modern cynicism as a form of nausea: "The cynic feels nauseated in principle: for him, everything is shit; his overdisappointed superego does not see the good in the shit."[74] This exaggerates the ferocity of modern cynicism once again; the problem with modern cynics, I would argue, is that they are not yet disappointed enough. This is how modern cynicism endures as a cultural phenomenon, avoiding ever reaching a point of crisis at which it might be confronted. Overstated though Sloterdijk's description of the modern cynic may be, it establishes a useful point of distinction with ancient Cynicism, where Cynic philosophers "are those who do not get nauseated." Sloterdijk suggests that ancient Cynics were like young children in this respect, "who do not yet know anything about the negativity of their excrement."[75] Here it might be worth giving ancient Cynics more credit. Cynic engagements with excrement can be understood as tactical rather than infantile (in the pejorative sense of that word), using the filth they produced to make a point. The scatological behavior of the ancient Cynic carries the message: "How funny it is that you find this so upsetting." For the self-consciously modern cynic, by contrast, the cynic who is determined to rise to the severe cynicism that Sloterdijk imagines, the lesson is transformed: "We are not yet nauseated enough." The lesson begins by addressing anyone who is prepared to hear—that is to say, anyone with even a nascent ecological consciousness—conveying what they already know, though the cynic puts things more harshly than most.

Humankind must face what it has become: "*a hyperproductive shit-accumulating industry-animal*," as Sloterdijk puts it with characteristic bluntness.[76] To point with uncomfortable insistence to this colossal production of waste is not the end of the matter, however, since waste production is tied into waste management. Even nausea can be co-opted. There is perhaps no better study of our ambivalent relation to waste than Dominique Laporte's much-neglected *History of Shit*. The rejection of waste is foundational to the production of order, Laporte argues, enforcing a "code of shitting—the master's code."[77] It will not suffice to point out the existence of all the shit we produce, so as to become better nauseated before the squalor. If that complaint is ever heard, it will lead to redoubled attempts to secure order, to redoubled industry, with the inevitable production of *more shit* as the problem of waste is again adopted by capital. Hence, a cynic of this more brazen, scatologically informed persuasion is not overcome by indignation that slides into morose sentiment at the sight of seas of plastic and a collapsing biosphere. This cynic does not point and stare and insist that something be done. Having long become familiar with the mutual circulation of shit and power, this cynic perceives the extent of the problem. Satisfied with nothing less than the annihilation of what we are, this cynic is not diverted in his or her radicalism by fond and sentimental illusions. This cynic occupies a position that suspects all action within the present order of existence to be at best a distraction, and at worst the means by which we accommodate ourselves to the status quo of global exploitation and degradation.

CODA: THE INEVITABILITY OF CYNICISM

As a result of recent scholarly interest in the phenomenon of Cynicism, there is a growing list of so-called inheritors of Cynic philosophy. Those identified as owing something to Cynicism in the premodern sense range from comedians and satirists,[1] to tricksters,[2] street artists,[3] and political activists such as the Russian punk collective Pussy Riot.[4] To this list we might add the case of Pyotr Pavlensky, who sewed his mouth shut in protest against the incarceration of members of Pussy Riot in 2012; had himself brought naked and wrapped in barbed wire to the main entrance of the Legislative Assembly of Saint Petersburg in 2013, and later that year nailed his scrotum to Red Square; cut off his earlobe while sitting naked on the roof of a prominent psychiatric hospital in 2014; and, after receiving asylum in France in 2017, set fire to the entrance of the Bank of France in Paris. Several parallels with

Cynic protest might be drawn: Pavlensky's public naked-ness; his shamelessness before that public; the high levels of endurance and self-control required in acts of public self-mutilation; his use of his body to manifest its truth (the truth of political oppression); his desire to "remain in Athens," so to speak ("Whenever I do a performance like this, I never leave the place. It's important for me that I stay there. The authorities are in a dead-end situation and don't know what to do"[5]); his commitment to "suck the authorities into his art,"[6] willing the state to involve itself, extricate him, and incarcerate him so that it may become an active if involuntary participant in the production of his art; his tactical co-option of the instruments of state power—the media, state propaganda, and psychiatry, for instance—to transmit, reflect, and amplify his message, where the basic facts cannot be distorted ("a chopped-off earlobe remains a chopped-off earlobe, a scrotum nailed to a square is always a scrotum nailed to a square"[7]); his adoption, embodiment, and intensification of the op-pressions he identifies; his claim to travel beyond those oppressions by way of them (once he has defied the au-thorities and succeeded in nailing himself to the ground, "the fear of pain, the fear of authority—dissolve," leading him to experience a "sense of liberation"); on a lower key, his attitude toward education ("I've studied at a number of places, from art schools to university, but I always leave before the end of the course. Why? Because I only need the information they have to offer. I have no need of any degree or diploma. What's a degree? It's just confirmation that you conformed to their standards entirely"[8]); his rejection of all forms of servitude (he describes art college as a "disciplinary institution that aims to make servants out of artists"[9]); his determination to puncture the "apathy, political indifference and fatalism of modern Russian society"[10] (which might be taken as a description of his opposition of something resembling ancient Cynicism to cynicism in the modern sense); and finally, in the case of the Bank of France, the ingratitude of the Cynic in exile to the host society ("We refused everything France wanted to give us"[11]). The parallels are stark. They suggest that Cynicism might yet have a role within contemporary society, though we should exercise caution when placing political activists and performance artists of such distinction and uniqueness within a Cynic framework if that Cynicism is not self-professed.

Various modern literary figures and musicians have also been studied in light of their apparent ancient and modern C/cynicisms, too numerous to be considered here.[12] The sheer number and range of writers and musicians identified presents its own problem, however. By some estimations, almost anyone who "does their own thing" might be considered a Cynic; "anarchists, tramps, hoboes, Beats, hippies, punks, new agers, bohemians"— the catalog goes on.[13] Though individual studies may avoid

such broad generalizations, outlining their own conceptions of cynicism with considerable care,[14] for a tradition
as diverse and multifaceted as Cynicism, the overall list
of authors, musicians, street artists, performance artists,
protestors, and activists who may or may not owe something to ancient or modern C/cynicism is likely to become
a long one. This may well be fertile ground for future research, but it is worth noting that most of those named
in the studies referred to above do not self-identify as C/
cynics. Though this book has limited its analysis of the
history of C/cynicism to cases of direct or indirect reference to the Cynics—an approach that may well have pre-
vented a broader understanding of the legacy of ancient
Cynic philosophy and the practices it inspired—this line
of argument does retain in view the awkward question
of what a self-avowed cynicism might look like today. It
raises the problem of what a more deliberate cynicism
might do, one that self-consciously draws from and seeks
to intensify contemporary cynic traits and dispositions
that are widespread but largely disavowed or dismissed.
This would be an attempt to push modern cynicism to realize and bring to fruition its own embedded but as yet
underdeveloped negativity. Given the endurance of earlier Cynicisms in later periods, this adoption and intensification of modern cynic traits might be accompanied by
the selective mimesis and further adaptation of ancient
Cynic technique, though with the caveat that any appeal

to older logics of transgression cannot return to the exact practices of ancient Cynicism. On this point, due attention to the improvised and contextually dependent nature of ancient Cynicism will ensure that attempts to learn from Cynicism are not reduced to straightforward exercises in mimicry. To take an obvious example: shitting before an audience will no longer have the same effect.[15] In part, this is because audiences have changed. They were essential to Cynic practice: "Diogenes, who needed very few things, nevertheless needed a crowd."[16] But audiences gather differently now. Shameless Cynic acts, performed by "quarrelsome figures ... capable of reacting in an uncivil way to the spectacle of false living,"[17] will find themselves received in part in a virtual context. In this setting, the rules of audience participation are altered, with spectators defining themselves online and at a distance by the indignation they express as they suck through teeth between successive tweets. Writing below the line; righteous indignation conceived as a reflex arc; intemperate but cursory reactions left as online traces: these are a function of the form. Unbridled anger has become a banal feature of online existence (or, in the terms of one of its severest critics, the distinguishing feature of the Web is that it allows people to remind one another on a daily basis that they are "awful pieces of shit"[18]). The Internet thrives on bad sentiment. Even rage directed against its main service providers will, if registered online, generate further revenue for the likes of Facebook, Twitter, and Google. If the Cynic causes a stir via social media, this is no marker of Cynic transgression. The visceral discomfort of a live audience gathered before the defecating Cynic has been replaced by a virtual audience that turns indignation into profit.

It is still worth taking up Sloterdijk's invitation to imagine a *"returned Diogenes"* climbing out of his Athenian tub into recent history, if only to measure the distance between his time and our own.[19] While Diogenes had taught "Be ready for anything," what he finds in our present seems beyond the grasp of Cynic subversion. It appears that in this very different context, acts of Cynic shamelessness no longer suffice to challenge social norms. All such perversions have been subsumed by psychologies that presume to treat them. There is even a so-called Diogenes's syndrome, which has to be the most ridiculous co-option of the name of Cynicism so far recounted in its pathologization of domestic squalor in the name of order and cleanliness. Given the mutually reinforcing development of psychiatry and carceral society, shameless acts of Cynic perversion designed to call into question the very values that animate the scandalized might only reinforce those very institutions that seek to normalize behavior by constructing abnormalities as sufficient reason for remedial action. The Cynic would be locked up, medicated, and worst of all, "understood."

The visceral discomfort of a live audience gathered before the defecating Cynic has been replaced by a virtual audience that turns indignation into profit.

The *modus operandi* of the ancient Cynic—to live differently—must also face its inevitable adoption by capital. Here the legacy of May 1968 serves as a useful reminder of how attempts to reinvent daily life can be outmaneuvered.[20] Everyday existence, as its critics claim, is now relentlessly exploited by capital.[21] Workers and educational subjects are expected to take upon themselves a stylization of life that will render them permanently adaptable to the whims of the marketplace. Individual lives are framed increasingly in this way, folded back on themselves, as lives of "self-stylization *vis-à-vis* the cultivation of [potentially counter-]cultural taste, body image and so forth."[22] When social problems are confronted, uncomfortable political questions are suspended "in the name of ethical immediacy." For instance, since the first Live Aid concert in 1985, a specific form of "ideological blackmail" has taken root, insisting that "caring individuals" can end famine directly by collectively reaching in their pockets, without the need for systemic reorganization.[23]

Should today's Cynic manage to avoid pathologization or arrest for indecency, his or her embodied practices would be perceived as just another lifestyle choice or political statement, another exhibitionist operating within the boundaries of liberal acceptability. Even the joyful exuberance of the Cynic may be co-opted, if we accept that the hegemonic model of late capitalism is no longer patriarchal in kind—that is to say, modeled after the Oedipal father who prohibits enjoyment—but is modeled on the obscene "primordial" father, the "Master of Enjoyment," who transforms the impulse to enjoyment into a repressive injunction.[24] The space of enjoyment is occupied by power, a power that insists its subjects gratify themselves. Absolute gratification is always withheld, of course, or placed just beyond reach, promised in each consumer good and life experience sold to its customers in order to develop a thirst rather than satisfy it. Given all of the above, a form of Cynicism modeled on its ancient ancestor would clearly struggle, its strategies no longer able to take effect, outmaneuvered by a political context that is permissive and even welcoming of deviance, or punitive but largely unshockable. Deviance has become legible to power—it has been given its place.

Any revival of Cynic philosophy will face a number challenges, then, and cannot be modeled on ancient Cynicism without considerable tactical adjustment. Here the Cynic commitment to a "straight life," outlined by Foucault, affords a good example of an approach that might be modified. The ancient Cynic took up a theme that underpinned ancient philosophy with the view to subverting it, ridiculing by co-option the true life or "straight life," the life that is undeviating in its pursuit of a certain *logos*. For respectable philosophy, the true life is indexed to a higher order. This is the life that is taught and legitimated in relation to whichever set of "human, social, and civic laws" a philosophy has alighted upon and recognized "as having to serve as the framework, grid, and organizing principle of the true life."[25] For the ancient Cynic, by contrast, the true life is forced to shed its attachment to higher things and is "indexed to nature."[26] As a transgressive act, this made tactical sense. By pursuing the "true life as other, scandalously other,"[27] the Cynic questions the principles by which "straightness" is judged. The Cynic makes tactical alliance with the so-called forces of nature, and pits them against every social convention he or she encounters. In modernity, however, this tactical alliance makes far less sense. Attempts to index a radical philosophy to nature, to natural forces, will quickly become entangled in a complex net of signification presided over by the human sciences. With the birth of biopolitics in the nineteenth century and its tightening grip on social life and political understanding throughout the twentieth, our conceptions of nature have become overburdened and potentially treacherous.[28] "Natural processes" are now recruited to operations of power as a matter of routine. Our self-understanding as beings subject to natural laws and tendencies has become, at least in part, a function of statistical analysis and population control. Besides, philosophy no longer teaches a "way of life" nor does it have any significant role offering social, political, and cultural counsel, however much its practitioners might choose to believe otherwise.[29] Released from the regulating effects of an erstwhile priesthood, a very different style of life rises to prominence: the life of pragmatic accommodations, instrumental maneuvers, and self-adjustments. In this context, the "straight life" of the Cynic philosopher would not function as an ironic and educationally fruitful exaggeration of a dominant mode of instruction, but would appear as if it were the product of some kind of residual dogmatism. The Cynic in pursuit of the straight or true life would seem quaint. Abandoning the straight life, then, the Cynic might instead take the dominant form of life—a life of broken promises and fragile ideals—and break it further, opting for the queer life, the life that is irrevocably bent; a life of gay outlaws, non-normative bodies, and abandoned futures.[30]

Though its traces are inevitably distorted, the provocations and impulses that ancient Cynicism set up remain in play. These include its historic attack on the idea of education and all forms of refinement, combined with its refusal to pretend that escape is possible, or social transformation meaningful, without a process of sustained, embattled enquiry committed to the internal unraveling of the systems it brings into question. Cynic philosophy demonstrates, by way of its immanent, performed critique, how deeply the Cynic remains fettered to the institutions he or she questions. In this respect, Cynic practice was geared as much toward a critique of the codependence of the transgressive practitioner and the culture to be subverted as it was to their separation. That codependence formed the paradox of transgression that the Cynic attempted to work through and overcome, by revealing how attempts to shed all the doubtful accruements of civilization would, if practiced within the society that the Cynic sought to transform, only cause the deliberately impoverished Cynic to be even more dependent on what Cynic critique derides. The highest achievements of civilized living, its kindest, most humane and beautiful procurements, remain suspect from a Cynic point of view. Sentiment is everywhere attacked for its cloaked operations of power. A Cynic critique is guided by its conviction that the worst excesses of civilization appear not despite its highest achievements, but can be located within, and by way of them. With all these lessons in mind, Cynicism teaches none of them. The active core of Cynicism remains evasive. It is to be located and lost in the tactical suppleness, in the refusal of Cynic practice to be identified with any one trait—the barrel, the farting, the free speech. Cynicism is a mode of revolt; it is the predicament of those who look about them and find everything wanting. A Cynic commitment to bring to existence "an *other* life", in Foucault's terms, is based on an unflinching critique of the life that we have, where nobody, not even the Cynic, can evade its transformative, scandalizing contempt. This commitment has nothing to do with the easy phrase "Another world is possible," which anyone may utter. The Cynic idea of an other life can be experienced only within this life as a scandal, as an offense to all standards of good taste and decency. Its alterity is felt by the offense it causes as it is gestured at, rather than argued for. The Cynic does not offer arguments that reason with themselves; that define their limits; that conclude and sum themselves up. A Cynic argument begins just as it ends— abruptly and without ceremony.

Ancient Cynic critique does not explain exactly what it finds repellent about society. A Cynic scandal does not supply the framework for understanding what informs and is ultimately intended by the Cynic act. Rather, the audience supplies the framework within which the scandal takes form as such. This occurs as that audience reacts to the Cynic act, mobilizing its own moral orders and economies of disgust through which it positions the Cynic and adjudicates upon the nature of the transgression it perceives. As we have seen, that interpretive framework will fail to adequately explain the Cynic and understand why the Cynic choses to act in this or that way, or at least, this is the effect Cynicism seeks to have by way of willfully bizarre, queer acts of transgression. That the Cynic is conversant with the appropriate norms and standards of behavior but decides to act otherwise is the key maneuver that ensures the Cynic remains incomprehensible. The audience may supply its framework of judgment, but still cannot comprehend why anyone should attempt to push at its borders without explaining what it is hoping to achieve. Extended to modern cynicism, and taking on board my claim that as

A Cynic argument
begins just as it
ends—abruptly and
without ceremony.

a cultural phenomenon our cynic predicament is the product of only partial dissatisfaction, that it is symptomatic of an aborted, unfulfilled nihilism, we might still wonder what a more complete, positively embraced contemporary cynic dissatisfaction would look like. Applying the logic of the ancient Cynic scandal to our own times, it seems that any embrace of present-day cynicism would not supply a more comprehensive, or better-articulated understanding, or explanation of why everything is bad and why cynicism is justified. Rather, it would focus on affirming its own amorphous but sustained sense of discontent. Like the ancient Cynic scandal, this is a bizarre choice, an affirmation of one's cynicism that must to some extent remain incoherent. Why affirm your cynicism? There is no adequate answer. But like ancient Cynicism, this affirmative act indicates the possibility of a different life, one that is predicated on the complete breakdown of this worldly existence, ranging from the destruction of its global economic orders of exploitation, pollution, and ecological collapse, to the radical adjustment of the subjectivities it has us occupy and exist within. This avowed modern cynic does not hope to inspire that breakdown any time soon, as if it would occur all at once in some kind of revolutionary singularity, but commits to the aggravating, inexplicable, yet transformative effects of an affirmed, affirmative cynicism. It need not model itself on the open aggression and confrontational presence of the ancient Cynic. Which is not to say that aggression and confrontation are ruled out. Modern cynics may opt for tactical confrontations; they may even howl once more in packs. In answer to the question: "Why riot?"[31] the cynic may respond, "Why not?" That is to say, the cynic expresses indifference before the question. For a nonconfrontational example of cynic practice, we might nonetheless turn to the "cynical reason of late socialism," which quietly preceded and prepared the way for the spectacular collapse of that social order.[32] This cynic outlook is well summed up by the following *anekdot*: "What is the difference between a Soviet pessimist and a Soviet optimist? A Soviet pessimist thinks that things can't possibly get any worse, but a Soviet optimist thinks that they will."[33] With similar optimism, the contemporary cynic picks up where the Soviet optimist left off. This cynic expends no effort arguing with the official discourses of the educated, industrious, and politically engaged, but greets them with a glance that is blank before inspection. Unresponsive to appeal, this glance confounds power and confronts it with its failure to organize a biddable cynicism.

Ancient Cynicism
The ancient Cynics were a loosely connected group of mendicant philosophers. They were easy to identify by their characteristic dress—the famous staff and cloak—their deliberate self-impoverishment, unrefined manners, lack of shame, perplexing behavior, and barking tone. These Cynics criticized the culture in which they found themselves by adopting a way of life designed to scandalize contemporaries, draw out their prejudices, and bear witness to the possibility of a completely different attitude to existence. It is distinguished from modern cynicism by the use of an uppercase "C."

Idealized Cynics
The ancient Cynics are only ever encountered second hand in the writing of those who were not themselves Cynics. To the extent that they were admired by subsequent commentators, this produced an idealized vision of Cynic philosophy that tended to downplay its most scandalous aspects and invert its lessons.

Insider cynics
A variant of modern cynicism (hence the lowercase "c"). Owing little if anything to ancient Cynicism, this category draws attention to the cynicism of contemporary professionals and public servants who believe that people are ultimately driven by selfish motives, and as a result of that point of view will do their best to survive within large organizations by dealing with their colleagues on those terms.

Master-cynics
Rich and powerful contemporary cynics who conceal their cynicism by adopting and instrumentalizing the values and beliefs of those over whom they wield power.

Modern cynicism

A general category used to refer to cynicism in all its modern forms. Said to be widespread, if not endemic to contemporary society, this cynicism ranges from the opportunistic and manipulative cynicism of the powerful—who will do anything to secure greater influence and wealth—right through to the abject cynicism of the oppressed and marginalized. It is distinguished from ancient Cynicism by the use of a lowercase "c."

Nihilism

In popular usage, nihilism is associated with the belief that life is meaningless and nothing is true. However, the term is also used in a less pejorative sense to describe the complex effects of a crisis of legitimation that typifies Western modernity, rendering the purposes of its political, cultural, and educational frameworks uncertain, and producing a range of distinctly fragile and conflicted subjectivities within which we are constrained to live.

Paternalistic cynicism

A form of modern cynicism that underpins the logic of government manipulation and institutional care. Particularly hard to detect because of its determined positivity, this is the cynicism of those who seek to shape public opinion by manipulating its already existing tendencies and habits. Though paternalistic cynics may often profit by way of the services they offer, this cynical attitude takes a more developed form as these activities are understood and justified, namely, as activities that will also apparently benefit those they manipulate.

Progressive cynicism

Like paternalistic cynicism, this is often hard to spot because of its insistent positivity. This form of cynicism is particularly prevalent among late modern educators who assume that education is underpinned by and can return to an essential goodness. Perpetuating a myth of educational redemption, this mode of cynicism must inevitably cause disappointment, look to apportion blame, and lead to an intensification of remedial action.

Strategic cynicism

This is the self-deluding, self-ennobling dream of today's university academic in particular, who is forever "strategic" in his or her interventions, arguing that it is necessary and prudent to consort with government and other influential agencies in the hope that such careful maneuvering will help loosen (though not break) the reins of power. It is the logic of studious academic compliance with agencies and systems academics are otherwise professionally trained to doubt. This species of academic, liberal-minded cynicism is hard to spot, since it is cloaked by good feeling and claims to beneficence. Its status is also built, rather oddly, on its disavowal of other more obvious cynicisms. It is based on the assumption, first of all, that modern cynicism is a feature of outright hypocrisy (the cynicism of those without scruples), or lack of faith (the cynicism of those given overly to pessimism), or second, that it is a product of disempowerment (the affliction of those in need of the uplifting influence of more education, often seen as a precursor to more meaningful engagement with democratic process). Like paternalistic and progressive cynicism, it is based on a series of dismissals that always locate the "cynicism" elsewhere.

Street Cynics

A much-derided ancient sect of mendicant preachers who associated with the poor and marginalized and roamed across the Roman Empire insulting the rich and powerful. Street Cynics were widely denounced as sham philosophers, though we know of them only through the perspective of philosophers and statesmen who attempted to counter street Cynicism with their own idealized conception of the Cynic legacy.

NOTES

Chapter 1

1. In German studies of C/cynicism, most notably Sloterdijk's famous *Critique of Cynical Reason* (*Kritik der zynischen Vernunft*) and Niehues-Pröbsting's *Der Kynismus des Diogenes und der Begriff des Zynismus*, the difference is reflected in the use of two distinct terms: *Kynismus* and *Zynismus*. The advantage of English usage is that it allows more easily for the gradual slippage of one into the other.

2. Sigmund Freud, *Civilization and Its Discontents*, in *The Standard Edition of the Complete Psychological Works of Sigmund Freud*, vol. 21, ed. James Strachey, trans. J. Strachey (London: Vintage, 2001), 100.

3. Freud, *Civilization and Its* Discontents, 100.

4. As depicted in *Thus Spoke Zarathustra*: "I love the great despisers, because they are the great reverers and arrows of yearning for the other shore" (Friedrich Nietzsche, *Thus Spoke Zarathustra: A Book for Everyone and Nobody*, trans. G. Parkes [Oxford: Oxford University Press, 2008], 13). The analogy might be extended further, where the modern cynic, by contrast, bears comparison to Nietzsche's last human: "There will come the time of the most despicable human, who is no longer able to despise itself" (Nietzsche, 15).

5. This focus is unusual within scholarship on the subject but has been a central aspect of my own engagement with it. See Ansgar Allen, *The Cynical Educator* (Leicester: Mayfly, 2017).

6. I would like to thank my three reviewers—David Mazella, Dan Taylor, and one who was anonymous—for generous feedback that contributed to the overall framing and direction of this book. Special thanks also to my editors at the MIT Press, Marc Lowenthal, Anthony Zannino, and Judy Feldmann, for inviting me to consider writing this book in the first place and for seeing it through to publication. I also acknowledge the PESGB for a fellowship that supported my initial forays into Cynicism of which this book is a belated output. My employer might also be credited for dislodging me from the quietude of my former office, and for prompting my own subsequent escape from an open-plan replacement to the nomadic existence of an academic exiled within his own institution. It has remained important to me under such conditions (which reflect only in a minor way the increasingly deplorable working conditions of the university sector) to question the origins of a widespread dissatisfaction

with education, which is so often the product of an overweening attachment to the value of the educated person, and a misplaced fondness for what education might otherwise be. I owe considerable thanks to Roy Goddard and Emile Bojesen, as well as Darren Webb, Matthew Clarke, Lindsay Miller, and Michael Miller, and above all Sarah Spencer, who would deny the accolade, but is a better Cynic than I will ever be. I dedicate this book to our children, Dylan and Sasha.

Chapter 2

1. Diogenes Laertius, *Lives of Eminent Philosophers*, volume 2, ed. Jeffrey Henderson, trans. R. D. Hicks, Loeb Classical Library (Cambridge, MA: Harvard University Press, 1931). In what follows I refer to Diogenes Laertius simply as Laertius, to avoid confusion with Diogenes of Sinope.

2. Donald R. Dudley, *A History of Cynicism: From Diogenes to the 6th Century AD* (London: Methuen, 1937), 87–89. Arguably, the phrase is already misleading since Cynicism was a practical rather than a theoretical philosophy.

3. See Laertius, *Lives of Eminent Philosophers*, 6.30–31.

4. Dudley, *History of Cynicism*, 24.

5. Dudley, 87.

6. Dudley, 88.

7. Laertius, *Lives of Eminent Philosophers*, 6.31.

8. In this reading, I also position myself against the argument that Cynic philosophy sought to "democratize" education, by basing its activity on an "open admissions" policy, as it moved the site of philosophical training from the "enclaves of classical philosophical schools" to the street (Kristen Kennedy, "Cynic Rhetoric: The Ethics and Tactics of Resistance," *Rhetoric Review* 18, no. 1 [1999]: 29). Although there is undoubtedly truth in this claim, for Cynicism did address a broader audience, in doing so it nonetheless submitted both education and philosophy to Cynic derision.

9. Peter Sloterdijk, *Critique of Cynical Reason*, trans. M. Eldred (Minneapolis: University of Minnesota Press, 2001); Michel Foucault, *The Courage of Truth: Lectures at the Collège de France 1983–1984*, trans. G. Burchell (Basingstoke: Palgrave Macmillan, 2011). Though Foucault's lectures have been influential on readings of Cynicism, they have not been available in their full, published form until relatively recently (since 2009 in French, and 2011 in English translation). Foucault's thought on Cynicism, published posthumously, appeared piecemeal at first, where an earlier version of Foucault's argument can be found within six lectures delivered at Berkeley in late 1983 and published in 2001 (*Fearless Speech* [Los Angeles: Semiotext(e), 2001], 115–133). For years

scholars were forced to rely on Flynn's summary of Foucault's final lectures (Thomas Flynn, "Foucault as Parrhesiast: His Last Course at the Collège de France (1984)," in *The Final Foucault*, ed. James Bernauer and David Rasmussen [Cambridge, MA: MIT Press, 1987]). As a result, the full influence of Foucault's analysis of Cynicism is perhaps yet to be felt. Long predating both Sloterdijk and Foucault is the study by Dudley, which is still used as a reference point: Dudley, *History of Cynicism*. Scholarly interest gained momentum during the 1970s, with a series of studies appearing, most notably Heinrich Niehues-Pröbsting, *Der Kynismus des Diogenes und der Begriff des Zynismus* (Munich: Fink, 1979). Throughout this book, for reasons of brevity and to simplify the exposition, I will keep in-text references to other authors, and the kind of intertextual debate that characterizes scholarly writing, to an absolute minimum. My sources are, however, fully acknowledged in the endnotes that follow.

10. See R. Bracht Branham, "Defacing the Currency: Diogenes' Rhetoric and the *Invention* of Cynicism," in *The Cynics: The Cynic Movement in Antiquity and Its Legacy*, ed. R. Bracht Branham and Marie-Odile Goulet-Gazé (Berkeley: University of California Press, 1996).

11. See R. Bracht Branham and Marie-Odile Goulet-Gazé, "Introduction," in *The Cynics*, 8.

12. Laertius, *Lives of Eminent Philosophers*, 6.48.

13. Pierre Hadot, *Philosophy as a Way of Life* (Oxford: Blackwell, 1995); *What Is Ancient Philosophy?* (Cambridge, MA: Harvard, 2004).

14. See David Mazella, *The Making of Modern Cynicism* (Charlottesville: University of Virginia Press, 2007), 36–42.

15. Ian Cutler, *Cynicism from Diogenes to Dilbert* (Jefferson, NC: McFarland, 2005), 25.

16. Martha Nussbaum, for example, engages in a brief discussion of Diogenes, who she quickly decides, offers a "flawed" example of the Socratic tradition with its focus on the "inner life of virtue and thought," and who has, for that reason, little to contribute to liberal humanism or philosophy more generally: "It is hard to know whether to grant Diogenes the title 'philosopher' at all, given his apparent preference for a kind of street theatre over Socratic questioning" (Martha Nussbaum, *Cultivating Humanity: A Classical Defense of Reform in Liberal Education* [Cambridge, MA: Harvard University Press, 1997], 57–58). John Cooper, to take another example, does not consider Cynicism worthy of inclusion in his survey of ancient philosophy since it does not provide "rationally worked out philosophical views" and so cannot be considered a philosophy in its own right. Cynicism, Cooper argues, should be studied under

the theme of "social history"; it should be treated as a "popular offshoot of philosophy," and need not trouble those who are concerned with serious philosophy (John M. Cooper, Pursuits of Wisdom: Six Ways of Life in Ancient Philosophy from Socrates to Plotinus [Princeton, NJ: Princeton University Press, 2012], 61–62).

17. For a summary of these positions see Bracht Branham and Goulet-Gazé, "The Cynics: Introduction," 21–23.

18. Bracht Branham, "Diogenes' Rhetoric and the Invention of Cynicism," 87.

19. Bracht Branham, 88–89.

20. And here perhaps Julian was right in attacking those who mimicked Cynic dress—the staff, cloak, and wallet—rather than Cynic philosophy. For an account of Julian's take on Cynicism, see chapter 4 of this volume.

21. Laertius, Lives of Eminent Philosophers, 6.22–23.

22. Seneca, Letters from a Stoic, trans. R. Campbell (London: Penguin, 2004), 176–177.

23. Seneca, Letters from a Stoic, 162.

24. Peter Brown, Power and Persuasion in Late Antiquity: Towards a Christian Empire (Madison: University of Wisconsin Press, 1992), 56. On this point something similar might be said of the customs and refinements of contemporary liberal democracies.

25. Brown, Power and Persuasion, 52.

26. Bracht Branham, "Diogenes' Rhetoric and the Invention of Cynicism," 89.

27. Mikhail Bakhtin, The Dialogic Imagination: Four Essays, trans. Caryl Emerson and Michael Holquist (Texas: University of Texas Press, 1981), 20.

28. Laertius, Lives of Eminent Philosophers, 6.38.

29. Erasmus wrote that "in this dog something of the divine must have been detected by Alexander the Great" (cited in Hugh Roberts, Dog's Tales: Representations of Ancient Cynicism in French Renaissance Texts [Amsterdam: Rodopi, 2006], 61).

30. Laertius, Lives of Eminent Philosophers, 6.32.

31. Foucault, Courage of Truth; Fearless Speech. See also Kennedy, "Cynic Rhetoric."

32. Bracht Branham, "Diogenes' Rhetoric and the Invention of Cynicism," 97.

33. Foucault, Fearless Speech, 127.

34. As I argue in Allen, Cynical Educator, 19–21.

35. Foucault, Fearless Speech, 126.

36. See especially Michel Foucault, The Will to Knowledge, trans. Robert Hurley (London: Penguin, 1998).

37. Diogenes, *Diogenes the Cynic: Sayings and Anecdotes* (Oxford: Oxford University Press, 2012), 10–11.

38. Foucault, *Courage of Truth*, 258.

39. Foucault, 194.

40. Plato, "Phaedo," in *The Last Days of Socrates*, trans. H. Tredennick and H. Tarrant (London: Penguin, 1993), 66b–c. It is worth noting that this dualism between the soul of the philosopher (which is inclined to reason) and his body (which operates as a source of material distraction), is elsewhere in Plato's corpus treated, Lloyd argues, as a "more complex location of the rational", where nonrational forces are placed "not outside a soul which is of itself entirely rational, but within the soul as a source of inner conflict" (Genevieve Lloyd, *The Man of Reason: "Male" and "Female" in Western Philosophy* [London: Routledge, 1993], 7). However, the contrast with the Cynic placement of the body nonetheless stands.

41. Foucault, *Courage of Truth*, 174 and *passim*.

42. Foucault, 173.

43. Foucault, 171.

44. Foucault, 222.

45. Foucault, 221–225.

46. Diogenes, *Sayings and Anecdotes*, 25.

Chapter 3

1. For a critique of the patriarchal constitution of Western philosophy, see Adriana Cavarero, *In Spite of Plato: A Feminist Rewriting of Ancient Philosophy* (Cambridge: Polity, 1995). See also Lloyd, *Man of Reason*.

2. Foucault, *Courage of Truth*, 272.

3. See Ben Knights, *The Idea of the Clerisy in the Nineteenth Century* (Cambridge: Cambridge University Press, 1978); Ian Hunter, *Rethinking the School: Subjectivity, Bureaucracy, Criticism* (New York: St. Martin's Press, 1994); Ian Hunter, *Culture and Government: The Emergence of Literary Education* (London: Macmillan, 1988).

4. For comparatively recent attempts at reviving, "updating," and giving new impetus to these ideas, see Andrew Delbanco, *College: What It Was, Is, and Should Be* (Princeton: Princeton University Press, 2011); Mark Edmundson, *Why Teach? In Defense of a Real Education* (New York: Bloomsbury, 2013); and William Deresiewicz, *Excellent Sheep: The Miseducation of the American Elite and the Way to a Meaningful Life* (New York: The Free Press, 2014). Interestingly, in her defense of liberal education, Martha Nussbaum engages in a brief discussion and dismissal of Diogenes (see note 16 in chapter 2, this volume).

Diogenes gets only a mention owing to the irritating fact (from the perspective of this tradition) that he is widely credited for inventing the concept of the cosmopolitan or "citizen of the world [or cosmos]" that (via the Stoics) later liberal thinkers have come to celebrate as a cultural ideal (Nussbaum, *Cultivating Humanity*, 56). Diogenes apparently coined the word when he declared that he was a cosmopolitan (Laertius, *Lives of Eminent Philosophers*, 6.63), a statement that is paralleled by the absurd (because unrealizable) notion that the "only true commonwealth" is that "which is as wide as the universe" (Laertius, 6.72). It has been argued that since the cosmos has no citizens, Diogenes's neologism could be understood as a "witty rejection of actual citizenship [including world citizenship] ... and an affirmation of the larger, apolitical allegiances of a Cynic," which refuse to be bound by such arbitrary constraints (Bracht Branham, "Diogenes' Rhetoric and the Invention of Cynicism," 96). The idea that anyone might be a citizen of the cosmos is patently absurd. To take these ideas in a more devious direction, then, Diogenes's neologism might be understood as a joke made at the expense of those who take citizenship seriously, those who extend their humanism to the most distant speck of dark matter hurtling through space. This includes all those who failed to understand the original jest and subsequently claim, in all seriousness, to uphold some cosmopolitan ideal, to be a citizen of the world.

5. Anthony Grafton and Lisa Jardine, *From Humanism to the Humanities: Education and the Liberal Arts in Fifteenth and Sixteenth-Century Europe* (London: Duckworth, 1986), xvi. For a recent collection critiquing this idea see Sam Ladkin, Robert McKay, and Emile Bojesen, eds., *Against Value in the Arts and Education* (London: Rowman & Littlefield, 2016).

6. Foucault, *Courage of Truth*, 278.

7. Diogenes, *Sayings and Anecdotes*, 24.

8. Foucault, *Courage of Truth*, 279.

9. Foucault, *Fearless Speech*, 131.

10. Dio Chrysostom cited in Foucault, *Fearless Speech*, 130.

11. A theme I explore in Allen, *Cynical Educator*. This builds on an argument that stems from my *Benign Violence: Education in and beyond the Age of Reason* (Basingstoke: Palgrave Macmillan, 2014).

12. Foucault, *Courage of Truth*, 279.

13. Foucault, *Fearless Speech*, 130.

14. Foucault, *Courage of Truth*, 280.

15. Foucault, *Courage of Truth*, 280.

16. Louisa Shea, *The Cynic Enlightenment: Diogenes in the Salon* (Baltimore: Johns Hopkins University Press, 2010), 10.

17. Shea, *Cynic Enlightenment*, 10.

18. Niehues-Pröbsting, *Der Kynismus des Diogenes und der Begriff des Zynismus*.

19. Shea, *Cynic Enlightenment*, 9.

20. Dudley, *History of Cynicism*, 54–55.

21. Bracht Branham and Goulet-Gazé, *The Cynics*. It has even been claimed that Diogenes at first misunderstood the prophecy by taking it too literally, an argument that is summarized in Kennedy, "Cynic Rhetoric," 28.

22. See Friedrich Nietzsche, *The Anti-Christ*, in *Twilight of the Idols and The Anti-Christ*, trans. R. J. Hollingdale (London: Penguin, 2003), §62. It is reasonably well-documented that Nietzsche drew inspiration from ancient Cynicism. His position in relation to Cynicism is complicated, however. Nietzsche can be found celebrating cynicism: "There is altogether no prouder and at the same time more exquisite kind of book than my books—they attain here and there the highest thing that can be attained on earth, cynicism" (*Ecce Homo: How One Becomes What One Is*, trans. R. J. Hollingdale [London: Penguin, 2004], 43). Describing *Ecce Homo*, Nietzsche announces: "I have now told my own story with a cynicism that will make history"—a project that anticipates, as he states, the "transvaluation of values" he has in mind (Christopher Middleton, ed., *Selected Letters of Friedrich Nietzsche* [Indianapolis, IN: Hackett, 1996], 326). Elsewhere, he denounces cynicism (though he may well be referring to a different cynicism here, using the term in its modern sense): "The oversaturation of an age with history ... leads an age into a dangerous mood of irony in regard to itself and subsequently into the even more dangerous mood of cynicism" (Friedrich Nietzsche, *Untimely Meditations*, trans. R. J. Hollingdale [Cambridge: Cambridge University Press, 1997], 83). This cynicism is, Nietzsche claims, the somewhat pleasurable refuge of those who "cannot endure the ironical state." It is a condition of surrender (*Untimely Meditations*, 107). There is the further difficulty (for interpreters at least) that some commentators have implicated Nietzsche in the birth (or at least entrenchment) of modern cynicism. See R. Bracht Branham, "Nietzsche's Cynicism: Uppercase or lowercase?" in *Nietzsche and Antiquity*, ed. Paul Bishop (New York: Camden House, 2004); Niehues-Pröbsting, *Der Kynismus des Diogenes und der Begriff des Zynismus*, 250–278; Sloterdijk, *Critique of Cynical Reason*, xxix. This is not the place for a detailed discussion of Nietzsche's cynicism (uppercase or lowercase), though in chapter 7 I do return to Nietzsche's diagnosis of modern nihilism—measuring its affinity to modern cynicism—and discuss his adaptation of the story of Diogenes and the lantern.

23. Foucault, *Courage of Truth*, 227.

24. Foucault, 244.

25. Foucault, 244.

26. Foucault, 245.

27. Foucault, 287.

28. Sloterdijk, *Critique of Cynical Reason*, 165.

29. Bracht Branham, "Diogenes' Rhetoric and the Invention of Cynicism," 96.

30. Sloterdijk, *Critique of Cynical Reason*, 151.

31. See how the choice of award was justified, as reported in the *New York Times*, October 24, 1969 (http://www.nytimes.com/books/97/08/03/reviews/beckett-nobel.html):

In a radio commentary on the choice of Mr. Beckett, Karl Ragnar Gierow, secretary of the academy, possibly mindful of the injunction in Alfred Nobel's will to honor uplifting literary works, seemed at pains to bring out the positive aspects of the deeply pessimistic Beckett. "The degradation of humanity is a recurrent theme in Beckett's writing," Dr. Gierow said, "and to this extent his philosophy, simply accentuated by elements of the grotesque and of tragic farce, can be said to be a negativism that knows no haven." But, using a photographic analogy, Dr. Gierow said that when a negative was printed, it produced "a positive, a clarification, with the black proving to be the light of day, the parts in deepest shade, those which reflect the light sources." The academy official continued: "The perception of human degradation is not possible if human values are denied. This is the source of inner cleansing, the life force in spite of everything, in Beckett's pessimism." Praising Mr. Beckett for "a love of mankind that grows in understanding as it plumbs further into the depths of abhorrence," Dr. Gierow concluded rhapsodically: "From that position, in the realms of annihilation, the writing of Samuel Beckett rises like a miserere from all mankind, its muffled minor key sounding liberation to the oppressed and comfort to those in need."

32. Dio Chrysostom, "Oration 8," in *The Cynic Philosophers from Diogenes to Julian*, ed. Robert Dobbin, trans. R. Dobbin (London: Penguin, 2012), 109.

33. Bracht Branham, "Diogenes' Rhetoric and the Invention of Cynicism," 103. For the distinction between Diogenes's rhetorical practice and a more conventional conception of rhetoric in which decorum performs a major role, see Kennedy, "Cynic Rhetoric."

34. Sloterdijk, *Critique of Cynical Reason*, 168.

35. Sloterdijk, 168.

36. Sloterdijk, 168.

37. Foucault, *Courage of Truth*, 253.

38. Foucault, 253.

39. Diogenes, *Sayings and Anecdotes*, 17.

40. Sloterdijk, *Critique of Cynical Reason*, 168 (emphasis in original).

41. Sloterdijk, 168.

42. Foucault, *Courage of Truth*, 262.

43. Foucault, 262.

44. Foucault, *Fearless Speech*, 139.

45. Foucault, 139.

46. Bakhtin, *Dialogic Imagination*, 23.

47. Bakhtin, 23.

48. Foucault, *Courage of Truth*, 165.

49. Bracht Branham, "Diogenes' Rhetoric and the Invention of Cynicism," 94. The syllogism in full: "All things belong to the gods. The wise are friends of the gods, and friends hold things in common. Therefore all things belong to the wise" (Laertius, Lives of Eminent Philosophers, 6.37).

50. Bracht Branham, 86.

51. Foucault, *Courage of Truth*, 208.

52. Foucault claims this attempt to reactualize the original core of a philosophy was essential to Platonism and Aristotelianism and was also present in Stoicism and Epicureanism, though in the latter attempts were also made to reactualize a form of existence. With Cynicism, the importance of reactualizing a form of existence almost completely replaces the drive to define oneself in relation to the essential doctrinal core of the tradition (see *Courage of Truth*, 209).

53. Foucault, 209.

54. Foucault, 209.

Chapter 4

1. Laertius, *Lives of Eminent Philosophers*, 6.21.

2. Laertius, 6.94.

3. Laertius, 6.84.

4. As argued in Dudley, *History of Cynicism*, 37.

5. Laertius, *Lives of Eminent Philosophers*, 6.82–83.

6. Menander quoted in Dudley, *History of Cynicism*, 41.

7. Stobaeus quoted in Dudley, 41.

8. Foucault, *Courage of Truth*, 210.

9. Mazella, *Making of Modern Cynicism*, 45.

10. Marcel Detienne and Jean-Pierre Vernant, *Cunning Intelligence in Greek Culture and Society*, trans. Janet Lloyd (Hassocks: Harvester Press, 1978).

11. James Romm, "Dog Heads and Noble Savages: Cynicism Before the Cynics?" in *The Cynics*. For an example of a pre-Socratic philosopher who has

also been identified as a Cynic precursor, see the Scythian philosopher Anacharsis, though the evidence for this is mixed, as discussed by R. P. Martin, "The Scythian Accent: Anacharsis and the Cynics," in *The Cynics*.

12. Margarethe Billerbeck, "The Ideal Cynic from Epictetus to Julian," in *The Cynics*, 205.

13. Foucault, *Courage of Truth*, 202.

14. It is worth noting that Cynicism was not entirely subsumed within Stoic philosophy. Zeno's associate Aristo of Chios succeeded in bringing out recessed Cynic traits, helping realign the Stoa with its roots in Cynic tradition. See J. I. Porter, "The Philosophy of Aristo of Chios," in *The Cynics*. Though some Stoics would attempt to expunge the Cynic influence from their tradition, it remained an awkward presence (see Dudley, *History of Cynicism*, 103).

15. J. M. Rist, *Stoic Philosophy* (Cambridge: Cambrige University Press, 1969), 54.

16. A. A. Long, "The Socratic Tradition: Diogenes, Crates, and Hellenistic Ethics," in *The Cynics*, 41.

17. Dudley, *History of Cynicism*, 118.

18. Bertrand Russell, *A History of Western Philosophy* (London: George Allen and Unwin, 1947), 256.

19. *The Oxford Companion to Philosophy*, 2nd ed., ed. Ted Honderich (Oxford: Oxford University Press, 2005), 185.

20. Shea, *Cynic Enlightenment*, 5.

21. Sloterdijk, *Critique of Cynical Reason*, 170.

22. Sloterdijk, 170.

23. There is no space here to place Epictetus's comments on Cynicism within the broader context of his philosophy. For this the reader may wish to consult A. A. Long, *Epictetus: A Stoic and Socratic Guide to Life* (Oxford: Oxford University Press, 2002).

24. Epictetus, "On Cynicism (Discourse 3. 22)," in *The Cynic Philosophers from Diogenes to Julian*, ed. Robert Dobbin, trans. R. Dobbin (London: Penguin, 2012), §80.

25. Derek Krueger, "The Bawdy and Society: The Shamelessness of Diogenes in Roman Imperial Culture," in *The Cynics*, 226.

26. "Without it he will be exposed to shame," Epictetus adds (Epictetus, "On Cynicism," §15). Contrast this with the argument I give in chapter 3 that shame and humiliation were key facets of Cynic philosophy.

27. Long, *Epictetus*, 50.

28. Long, 13.

29. See Long, 10–12.

30. Epictetus, "On Cynicism," §10–11.

31. Epictetus, §89.

32. Dudley, *History of Cynicism*, 194.

33. Epictetus, "On Cynicism," §93.

34. Epictetus cited in Dudley, *History of Cynicism*, 51.

35. Ethel M. Kersey, *Women Philosophers: A Biocritical Sourcebook* (New York: Greenwood Press, 1989), 132.

36. John Moles, "'Honestius Quam Ambitiosius'? An Exploration of the Cynic's Attitude to Moral Corruption in His Fellow Men," *Journal of Hellenic Studies* 103 (1983): 111. A similar claim (with the accompanying suggestion that Cynics were committed to "class emancipation") is made by Kennedy, "Cynic Rhetoric," 30; Kennedy, "Hipparchia the Cynic: Feminist Rhetoric and the Ethics of Embodiment," *Hypatia* 14, no. 2 (1999).

37. As recounted by Laertius in a short section devoted to Hipparchia, a section which cannot even maintain its own focus but ends by discussing what became of her husband (Laertius, *Lives of Eminent Philosophers*, 6.96–6.99).

38. Laertius, 6.96.

39. This is an idea that frames Michèle Le Doeuff's book-length essay concerning women and philosophy: Michèle Le Doeuff, *Hipparchia's Choice* (New York: Columbia University Press, 2007).

40. Laertius, *Lives of Eminent Philosophers*, 6.12.

41. Laertius, 6.3.

42. Laertius, 6.72.

43. Mazella, *Making of Modern Cynicism*, 232. Here Mazella draws from a study by Morgan, where in one such lesson Diogenes can be encountered remarking upon the practice of "Ethiopian shitting," as if he were not himself inclined to move from commentary to the act itself (Teresa Morgan, *Literate Education in the Hellenistic and Roman Worlds* [Cambridge: Cambridge University Press, 1998], 186).

44. Lucian, "The Passing of Peregrinus," in *Lucian*, volume 5, ed. Jeffrey Henderson, trans. A. M. Harmon (Cambridge, MA: Harvard University Press, 1936).

45. Lucian, *The Runaways*, in *Lucian*, volume 5, §16.

46. Lucian, *The Runaways*, §21.

47. Lucian, "Demonax," in *Lucian*, volume 1, ed. Jeffrey Henderson, trans. A. M. Harmon (Cambridge, MA: Harvard University Press, 1913). "Apparent" because Lucian was a notorious satirist and dissembler—it is hard to tell if Demonax was real or imagined (see Diskin Clay, *Lucian of Samosata: Four Philosophical Lives (Nigrinus, Demonax, Peregrinus, Alexander Pseudomantis)*, ed. Wolfgang Haase, vol. II.36.5, [Berlin: Walter de Gruyter, 1992];

Denis M. Searby, "Non-Lucian Sources for Demonax with a new collection of 'fragments,'" *Symbolae Osloenses* 83, no. 1 [2008]). Idealized, because of the "straight, sane, irreproachable life" he was said to lead (Lucian, "Demonax," 145): "Probably he had most in common with Socrates," Lucian continues, "although he seemed to follow the man of Sinope [i.e.. Diogenes]. ... He did not, however, alter the details of his life in order to excite the wonder and attract the gaze of men he met, but led the same life as everyone else ... and played his part in society and politics." His conversations were, moreover, full of "Attic charm" and his visitors "did not feel contempt for him because he was ill-bred or aversion to his criticisms ... but were beside themselves for joy and were far better, happier and more hopeful of the future" as a result. He was "never known to make an uproar" and though he would rebuke others for their sins (often with a good dose of humor), he "forgave" them too, "thinking that one should pattern after doctors, who heal sicknesses but feel no anger for the sick" (147). Demonax was a great reconciler, consoler of others, and even pacifier: "On occasion, he has talked reason to excited mobs, and has usually persuaded them to serve their country in a temperate spirit. ... Such was the character of his philosophy—kind, gentle and cheerful" (149.).

48. Lucian, "On Salaried Posts in Great Houses," in *Lucian*, volume 3, ed. Jeffrey Henderson, trans. A. M. Harmon (Cambridge, MA: Harvard University Press, 1921), 435. Later in life Lucian was employed in service of the emperor in Egypt, a highly lucrative position. Rebutting possible accusations of hypocrisy, he clarifies that in his earlier essay, "I did not say that all wage-earners lived a mean and petty existence: no, it was those in private houses who endured slavery under the pretext of education that I pitied" ("Apology for the 'Salaried Posts in Great Houses,," in *Lucian*, volume 6, ed. Jeffrey Henderson, trans. K. Kilburn [Cambridge, MA: Harvard University Press, 1959]). Lucian argues that cultured men and lovers of philosophy such as himself should not be shy of earning a living nor serving in public office; it does not diminish them to place themselves in service of imperial power.

49. Mazella, *Making of Modern Cynicism*, 43.

50. R. Bracht Branham, *Unruly Eloquence: Lucian and the Comedy of Traditions* (Cambridge, MA: Harvard University Press, 1989), 14.

51. Bracht Branham, *Unruly Eloquence*, 15.

52. Bracht Branham, 19. Branham argues that Lucian's characters "are not meant to be credible"—and here Menippus is no exception—but offer him a "flexible pretense" that "serves to provoke, joke, speculate, amuse" (20.). There is no attempt to rise to their example, or revitalize the teaching of individual philosophers who were in some cases five centuries gone. Lucian draws from a

common stock of ancient characters, including Cynics. His satirical form may play one ancient tradition off another, often at the expense of those he depicts, but, as Branham argues, this was "itself recreative for author and audience" alike. It allowed that audience to recognize itself within the cultural tradition it inherits. Indeed, Lucian's humor depended on a high level of shared understanding of ancient Greek culture in order to take effect 212–214.). With philosophy having become "an accepted element in the self-image of the [second century] ruling class," and with it being "materially advantageous to have a veneer of philosophical culture" (121), Lucian's satire served up so many in jokes, prompting laughter as an expression of refinement.

53. Sloterdijk, *Critique of Cynical Reason*, 172.

54. Foucault, *Courage of Truth*, 195.

55. Sloterdijk, *Critique of Cynical Reason*, 172.

56. Sloterdijk, 174. As Bracht Branham argues, Lucian was eager to assert his credentials as a rhetor and man of *paideia*, being "perfectly aware of his status as an outsider" with humble beginnings, who has traveled to Athens and now finds himself at the "centre of an antique and intensely discriminating literary culture." In a manoeuvre that seems to bear more relation to the modern conception of a cynic as a self-interested, unprincipled operator, Lucian sought to "convert the fact of his dubious origins to rhetorical advantage; thus he consistently associates himself with esteemed outsiders such as the legendary 'barbarians' ... or 'respectable aliens' such as the Cynics ... while simultaneously embedding his literary values in a cluster of respected traditions" stemming from classical authors such as Plato and Aristophanes (Bracht Branham, *Unruly Eloquence*, 32).

57. Sloterdijk, 172.

58. Julian, "To the Cynic Heracleios," in *The Cynic Philosophers from Diogenes to Julian*, ed. Robert Dobbin, trans. R. Dobbin (London: Penguin, 2012), 199.

59. Foucault, *Courage of Truth*, 202.

60. Julian, "To the Cynic Heracleios" (Penguin ed.), 195.

61. " You have even managed to diminish the prestige of philosophy in general," was how Emperor Julian put it, clearly incensed (Julian, 200).

62. Julian, 195.

63. Dudley, *History of Cynicism*, 125–141.

64. See Brown, *Power and Persuasion in Late Antiquity*.

65. Julian, "To the Cynic Heracleios" (Penguin ed.), 194.

66. Julian, "To the Uneducated Cynics," in *The Works of the Emperor Julian*, volume 2, ed. Jeffrey Henderson, trans. W. C. Wright (Cambridge, MA: Harvard University Press, 1913), 49.

67. Julian, "To the Cynic Heracleios" (Penguin ed.), 194.

68. Julian, "To the Uneducated Cynics," 49.

69. Julian, "To the Uneducated Cynics." Elsewhere translated as *Against the Ignorant Cynics*.

70. Julian, "Against the Ignorant Cynics," 188.

71. Julian, "To the Cynic Heracleios" (Penguin ed.), 194.

72. Julian, "To the Uneducated Cynics," 59.

73. Julian, "To the Uneducated Cynics," 61.

74. Julian, "To the Cynic Heracleios" (Penguin ed.), 194.

75. For the unabridged argument see "To the Cynic Heracleios," in *The Works of the Emperor Julian*, volume 2, 99–119.

76. Where the distinction between medicine (occupied with the body) and philosophy (occupied with the soul) was yet to be made.

77. Julian, "To the Cynic Heracleios" (Loeb ed.), 79–81. Here, the work of the second-century philosopher and physician Galen is worth looking at for a detailed account of how a philosopher-teacher should occupy a subordinate position involving moral exhortation. See Galen, *On the Passions and Errors of the Soul* (Columbus: Ohio State University Press, 1963). See my summary of Galen's argument in Allen, *Cynical Educator*, 43–45, which draws from Michel Foucault, *The Hermeneutics of the Subject: Lectures at the Collège de France 1981–1982*, trans. G. Burchell (Basingstoke: Palgrave Macmillan, 2005), 396–399.

78. Cited in Billerbeck, "Ideal Cynic," 216. For a slightly different translation see: Julian, "To the Cynic Heracleios" (Penguin ed.), 201; "To the Cynic Heracleios" (Loeb ed.), 129.

79. Julian, "Against the Ignorant Cynics," 187.

80. Julian, "To the Cynic Heracleios" (Penguin ed.), 201.

81. Such indeed is the "Neoplatonic coloring" of Julian's speech (Billerbeck, "Ideal Cynic," 216).

82. Julian, "To the Cynic Heracleios" (Penguin ed.), 201.

83. Julian, "To the Cynic Heracleios" (Penguin ed.), 194.

84. Foucault, *Courage of Truth*, 181. Dudley makes a similar argument: Dudley, *History of Cynicism*, 209–213.

85. Foucault, *Courage of Truth*, 182. Direct comparison between Cynics and Franciscans can be found in Renaissance texts describing the order (see Sylvain Matton, "Cynicism and Christianity from the Middle Ages to the Renaissance," in *The Cynics*, 254–255, and within the writings of Franciscans and Dominicans themselves [252–253]).

86. Foucault, *Courage of Truth*, 183.

87. Sloterdijk, *Critique of Cynical Reason*, 158.

88. Leif E. Vaage, "Like Dogs Barking: Cynic Parrēsia and Shameless Asceticism," *Semeia* 57 (1992): 32.

89. Vaage, "Like Dogs Barking," 38.

90. Foucault, *Courage of Truth*, 262.

91. See, in particular, F. Gerald Downing, *Cynics, Paul and the Pauline Churches* (London: Routledge, 1998); *Cynics and Christian Origins* (Edinburgh: T&T Clark, 1992); *Christ and the Cynics: Jesus and Other Radical Preachers in First-Century Tradition* (Sheffield: Sheffield Academic Press, 1988); John Dominic Crossan, *The Historical Jesus: The Life of a Mediterranean Jewish Peasant* (New York: Harper Collins, 1992); Burton L. Mack, *The Lost Gospel: The Book of Q and Christian Origins* (New York: HarperCollins, 1993); *A Myth of Innocence: Mark and Christian Origins* (Philadelphia: Fortress Press, 1988); Leif E. Vaage, *Galilean Upstarts: Jesus' First Followers According to Q* (Valley Forge, PA: Trinity Press, 1994). For a summary critique of this research trajectory, see Hans Dieter Betz, "Jesus and the Cynics: Survey and Analysis of a Hypothesis," *Journal of Religion* 74, no. 4 (1994); Paul Rhodes Eddy, "Jesus as Diogenes? Reflections on the Cynic Jesus Thesis," *Journal of Biblical Literature* 115, no. 3 (1996). And for responses, see F. Gerald Downing, "Deeper Reflections on the Jewish Cynic Jesus," *Journal of Biblical Literature* 117, no. 1 (1998); David Seeley, "Jesus and the Cynics Revisited," *Journal of Biblical Literature* 116, no. 4 (1997).

92. Crossan, *Historical Jesus*.

93. Bernhard Lang, "Jesus among the Philosophers: The Cynic Connection Explored and Affirmed, with a Note on Philo's Jewish-Cynic Philosophy," in *Religio-Philosophical Discourses in the Mediterranean World*, ed. Anders Klostergaard Petersen and Georg van Kooten (Leiden: Brill, 2017).

94. Seeley, "Jesus and the Cynics Revisited," 709–711.

95. Crossan, *Historical Jesus*, 421.

96. Vaage, *Galilean Upstarts*, 106.

97. Krueger, "Shamelessness of Diogenes in Roman Imperial Culture," 229. Downing's response to this criticism (Downing, *Cynics, Paul and the Pauline Churches*, 41–48), makes the case for a less scatological Cynicism, but in so doing confirms the argument that studies of early Christian Cynicism draw from the slightly more "respectable" side of the Cynic tradition.

98. Downing, "Deeper Reflections on the Jewish Cynic Jesus," 99.

99. See Krueger, "Shamelessness of Diogenes in Roman Imperial Culture," 236–237.

100. Gail Paterson Corrington, "The Defense of the Body and the Discourse of Appetite: Continence and Control in the Greco-Roman World," *Semeia* 57 (1992).

101. In what follows I draw from Derek Krueger, *Symeon the Holy Fool: Leontius's Life and the Late Antique City* (Berkeley: University of California Press, 1996), 72–89; "Diogenes the Cynic among the Fourth Century Fathers," *Vigiliae Christianae* 47, no. 1 (1993); "Shamelessness of Diogenes in Roman Imperial Culture."

102. Krueger, *Symeon the Holy Fool*, 81.

103. See Krueger, *Symeon the Holy Fool*, 81. The influence of Diogenes on Leontius's account remains a point of contention. For a countervailing view see, Vincent Déroche, *Études sur Léontios de Néapolis* (Upsalla: Upsalla Universitet, 1995), 195–197; Sergey A. Ivantov, *Holy Fools in Byzantium and Beyond* (Oxford: Oxford University Press, 2006), 108.

104. Krueger, "Shamelessness of Diogenes in Roman Imperial Culture," 239. Renaissance compilations, such as Erasmus's translation of Plutarch's *Apophthegmata* (1531), performed a similar function, though with moralizing Christian overtones. See Roberts, *Dog's Tales*, 63–68.

105. See Krueger, *Symeon the Holy Fool*, 19–35.

106. Systematic shortening and paraphrasing of the life of Symeon would nonetheless follow in the tenth century, with subsequent accounts "concerned to provide the Church with versions of the lives of the saints acceptable for use during worship services." As these accounts were brought into conformity with one another, the life of Symeon was sanitized and simplified (see Krueger, *Symeon the Holy Fool*, 52–55).

107. Krueger, 103.

108. Krueger, 96–99.

109. Krueger, 20.

110. Krueger, 40.

111. Krueger, 41.

112. Leontius in Krueger, 132–133.

113. Krueger, 49.

114. Broadly, this is the interpretation Krueger offers. On living in accord with virtue rather than nature, see Krueger, 107. For an overall summary of Krueger's argument, see 126–129.

115. Krueger, 49.

Chapter 5

1. Matton, "Cynicism and Christianity," 240.

2. For an account of Renaissance sources see Roberts, *Dog's Tales*, 33–54.

3. Matton, "Cynicism and Christianity," 243.

4. Augustine, *Concerning the City of God against the Pagans*, trans. Henry Bettenson (London: Penguin, 2003), 581.

5. Dudley ends his account in the sixth century, concluding that with the rise of Christianity and the transfer of Cynic ideas to Christian ascetics, "Cynicism [in the ancient sense, as a lived philosophy] had nothing further to offer mankind" (*History of Cynicism*, 208).

6. Matton, "Cynicism and Christianity," 244.

7. See Matton, 246.

8. Matton, 248–49.

9. Gaguin cited in Matton, 249.

10. Matton, 248–49.

11. Mario Equicola cited in Matton, 250.

12. See Matton, 251–52.

13. See Matton, 252–54.

14. Jean de Gerson cited in Matton, 257.

15. Gabriel Du Préau cited in Matton, 258.

16. Matton, 259–261.

17. Matton, 262–264.

18. See Roberts, *Dog's Tales*; Michéle Clément, *Le Cynisme à la Renaissance d'Érasme à Montaigne* (Geneva: Droz, 2005); Niklaus Largier, *Diogenes der Kyniker: Exempel, Erzählung, Geschichte in Mittelalter und früher Neuzeit. Mit einem Essay zur Figur des Diogenes zwischen Kynismus, Narrentum und postmoderner Kritik* (Tübingen: Max Niemeyer Verlag, 1997). Roberts argues, against Clément, that although reference to Cynicism, in particular Diogenes, can be found strewn across Renaissance texts, there was no neo-Cynic movement in Renaissance Europe. There is too much variation in the influence of Cynicism, with individual episodes from the life of Diogenes subject to multiple interpretations. Highly idealized Christian readings were less prominent by comparison to the medieval period, but the appeal of the dogs was nonetheless "often tempered by dismay at their shamelessness." Hence, though "we encounter a series of extraordinary representations of the Cynics ... the Dogs themselves, and their philosophy, are forever out of sight" (Roberts, *Dog's Tales*, 273–274). Rabelais appears more amenable to the more challenging sides of Cynic philosophy, but this was tempered in its own way, as considered below.

19. François Rabelais, *The Complete Works of Doctor François Rabelais Abstractor of the Quintessence: Being an Account of the Inestimable Life of the Great Gargantua, and of the Herioc Deeds, Sayings and Marvellous Voyages of His Son the*

Good Pantagruel, volume 1, trans. Sir Thomas Urquhart and Peter Motteux (London: Bodley Head, 1933), xxxv.

20. Rabelais, *Complete Works*, volume 1, 404.

21. Roberts, *Dog's Tales*, 170.

22. Rabelais, *Complete Works*, volume 1, 427. For a collection of other brief appearances, see Roberts, *Dog's Tales*, 189–191.

23. Roberts, *Dog's Tales*, 171–189.

24. Edwin M. Duval, *The Design of Rabelais's Tiers Livre de Pantagruel* (Geneva: Droz, 1997), 15–16.

25. Roberts, *Dog's Tales*, 173.

26. Roberts, 166.

27. Roberts, 166.

28. Lucian, "How to Write History," trans. A. M. Harmon, in *Lucian*, volume 5, ed. Jeffrey Henderson, Loeb Classical Library. (Cambridge, MA: Harvard University Press, 1936), 3.

29. Laertius, *Lives of Eminent Philosophers*, 6.48.

30. There could be a simple explanation: furnishing Diogenes with books and suchlike may simply be a comic device to contrast Diogenes the contemplative philosopher with Diogenes the tub-roller, as argued in Roberts, *Dog's Tales*, 178.

31. Here I go further than Roberts who does not consider the discussion of barrel-rolling to have a particularly subversive message intended to ridicule the activities of a frantic and fearful citizenry. Roberts makes the more moderate claim that the discussion of barrel-rolling allows Rabelais to meditate on "the writer's role in society" (as someone who seeks to contribute positively, though he has little to offer but his writing), allowing him to make a "courageous claim to joyousness even at times of hardship and conflict" (Roberts, 188). Bakhtin makes a similar point, arguing that the episode conveys the message: "No one should be idle, but laughter is not an idle occupation"—so let Diogenes roll his barrel, because in that comic act he "defends the rights of laughter which must prevail even in the most serious historic struggle". His barrel-rolling, Bakhtin argues, is "opposed not to the heroic citizens of Corinth but to the gloomy calumniators, to the enemies of free humor" (Mikhail Bakhtin, *Rabelais and His World*, trans. Helene Iswolsky [Bloomington: Indiana University Press, 1984], 178–179). It is worth noting, as an aside (and perhaps in support of Roberts's position), that during the Renaissance the barrel-rolling episode was a literary commonplace (Roberts, *Dog's Tales*, 191–199), and was generally used without great irony and with a tendency to

self-depreciation (in effect: "Though I desired to be of assistance to the common weal, perhaps all I've achieved is a little barrel-rolling").

32. Rabelais, *Complete Works*, volume 1, 436.

33. Rabelais, 435.

34. See Allen, *Cynical Educator*, 178–187.

35. Bakhtin, *Rabelais and His World, passim*.

36. Bakhtin, 19–20.

37. Bakhtin, 47–49.

38. Bakhtin, *Dialogic Imagination*, 239–240.

39. Roberts, *Dog's Tales*, 280.

40. As argued in Terry Eagleton, "The Subject of Literature," *Cultural Critique* 2 (1985).

41. Eagleton, "Subject of Literature," 99.

42. Eagleton, 101.

43. Bakhtin, *Dialogic Imagination*, 239.

44. Rabelais, *Complete Works*, volume 1, 147–150.

45. Rabelais, 380.

46. See Roberts, *Dog's Tales*, 187–188.

47. Bakhtin, *Rabelais and His World*, 188.

48. Mazella, *Making of Modern Cynicism*, 50–51.

49. Mazella, 49.

50. See Roberts, *Dog's Tales*, 55–158.

51. See Mazella, *Making of Modern Cynicism*, 49.

52. David Hershinow, "Cash Is King: Timon, Diogenes, and the Search for Sovereign Freedom," *Modern Philology* 115, no. 1 (2017): 59. It is worth noting how the "fantasy" of sovereign frankness would fall away as rhetoric lost its position of preeminence in the mid- to late seventeenth century. Rhetoric declined during what has been described as "the general humiliation of elite culture" that occurred when (to put it bluntly) classical training "proved incapable of keeping Charles I's head attached to his body." The educated elites were provoked to "reassess the effectiveness of a classical eloquence [found in rhetoric] that had once served as the primary verbal armory for projecting, defending, and sustaining power in early modern England" (Mazella, *Making of Modern Cynicism*, 82). As part of this reassessment, the role of Cynic frankness at court became uncertain, so that, following the Restoration of the English monarchy, new strategies were required to protect power against incursions from below. For an account of a rather different, but once again conservative early modern use of Diogenes, see Deann Armstrong, "Hanging the Watch:

Erotic Timekeeping and Temporal Cynicism in *The Roaring Girl*," *Modern Philology* 116, no. 2 (2018). Armstrong explores how Diogenes was associated with freedom from lust, among other things (since he satisfied his desire alone), and as such was harnessed to a critique of the theater, viewed by its detractors as a dangerous pastime, a "technology of deceit and feminization" (if not "the beginning of whoredome") that allowed nonnormative pleasures and ideas to be entertained without due restraint. This was coincident with Diogenes's widespread depiction in early modern England as a misogynist, where the appeal Diogenes makes to nature is interpreted as sanctioning unambiguous manliness and consequent superiority (see again Armstrong).

53. Mazella, *Making of Modern Cynicism*, 53–55.

54. Mazella, 55.

55. Mazella, 72.

56. Hershinow, "Cash Is King."

57. See Mazella, *Making of Modern Cynicism*, 75. See also Hershinow, "Cash Is King," and the brief analysis by Karl Marx, "Economic and Philosophical Manuscripts (1844)," in *Early Writings*, trans. Rodney Livingstone and Gregor Benton (London: Penguin, 1975), 376–377.

58. Mazella, *Making of Modern Cynicism*, 74–75.

59. David Hershinow, "Diogenes the Cynic and Shakespeare's Bitter Fool: The Politics and Aesthetics of Free Speech," *Criticism* 56, no. 4 (2014).

60. Hershinow, "Diogenes the Cynic," 821.

61, Hershinow, 826.

62. Hershinow, 827.

63. See Mazella, *Making of Modern Cynicism*, 67–70.

64. Joseph Hall, cited in R. W. Ingram, *John Marston* (Boston: Twayne Publishers, 1978), 25–26.

65. John Marston, *The Scourge of Villanie 1599*, ed. G. B. Harrison (London: Bodley Head, 1925), v.

66. Mazella, *Making of Modern Cynicism*, 69–70. Hence Mazella's argument: "Though Marston's writing has been criticized because his claims as a moral censor seem bizarrely mismatched with his obscene style, his lapses in decorum are better understood as symptoms of the corruptions he depicts ... through his breakdowns in style" (70). Broadly analogous objections have been placed at the door of much later writers such as Friedrich Nietzsche, who may be defended along similar lines, as may a writer such as Thomas Bernhard (famously accused for being a *Nestbeschmutzer*); I would argue that none comes off worse than Bernhard's supercilious narrator in his vicious monologues against the state of contemporary society. In modernity, the educated

critic who finds everything wanting is apparently doomed to this self-debasing strategy. See my essays on Nietzsche and the critique of the educated in Ansgar Allen, "Awaiting Education: Friedrich Nietzsche on the Future of Our Educational Institutions," *Philosophical Inquiry in Education* 24, no. 2 (2017); "The End of Education: Nietzsche, Foucault, Genealogy," *Philosophical Inquiry in Education* 25, no. 1 (2018). For a countervailing view, that "to identify Marston with the sometimes hysterical [violent and unstable] satirist of his poems is to rule out the possibility that he was self-consciously cultivating a pose," and that Marston is for that reason, somehow unaffected by the malaise he narrates, see Anthony Caputi, *John Marston, Satirist* (Ithaca, New York: Cornell University Press, 1961), 2.

Chapter 6

1. Mazella, *Making of Modern Cynicism*, 82.

2. As argued in Mazella, 83.

3. On the marginalization of Cynicism from the history of philosophy, see Heinrich Niehues-Pröbsting, "The Modern Reception of Cynicism: Diogenes in the Enlightenment," in *The Cynics*, 330–331. Cynicism had always occupied a marginal position in relation to the other philosophical schools, and yet remained connected to this tradition so long as philosophy was understood to be in part a biographical matter, where the exemplary life of the philosopher "was considered the verification of the doctrine," as Niehues-Pröbsting puts it. In modernity, this biographical element is itself marginalized, so that "only the theoretical products of philosophers, not their biographies, are of importance for the history of philosophy" (Niehues-Pröbsting, 330). This leads to the dismissal of Cynicism from the philosophical canon for its lack of theoretical content, and for its reliance upon biographical details and anecdotes of doubtful authenticity.

4. See Allen, *Cynical Educator*, 97.

5. Allen, 89–104.

6. Mazella, *Making of Modern Cynicism*, 104–109.

7. The "insider cynic" is part of a taxonomy of cynicism described in Alan Keenan, "Twilight of the Political? A Contribution to the Democratic Critique of Cynicism," *Theory & Event* 2, no. 1 (1998).

8. Mazella, *Making of Modern Cynicism*, 9–10. Here Mazella draws from but also develops Keenan's briefly outlined taxonomy of modern cynicism, in which Keenan distinguishes between "master-cynics," "disempowered insiders," and finally, the "disempowered outsider," who becomes the focus of his analysis of political disaffection (Keenan, "Twilight of the Political?").

9. The conventional view is to associate Trump's rise to power with the cynicism of the "disempowered outsider" (in Keenan's terms), which is to say that Trump succeeded because of a loss of faith in conventional politics that was allowed to set in among those who were most disadvantaged by the American political system. What most confuses those who do not see themselves as cynics of this variety, or at least, those who do not place themselves within this demographic, is that Trump drew votes from elsewhere, too. As I boarded a plane on the morning of Trump's victory, the person before me summed up this state of confusion very well: "What I cannot understand," he said on his phone, "is that educated people voted for him too."

10. Lyttelton, cited in Mazella, *Making of Modern Cynicism*, 106.

11. Lyttelton, cited in Mazella, 106.

12. As an intervening form in the reduction of Cynicism to "mass cynicism," Mazella argues," the Cynic was transformed from an opponent of the mob to one of its most dangerous leaders (84).

13. Niehues-Pröbsting, "Modern Reception of Cynicism," 332.

14. Mazella, *Making of Modern Cynicism*, 143–162.

15. See Niehues-Pröbsting, "Modern Reception of Cynicism"; *Der Kynismus des Diogenes und der Begriff des Zynismus*; Mazella, *Making of Modern Cynicism*; Shea, *Cynic Enlightenment*; and Sharon Stanley, *The French Enlightenment and the Emergence of Modern Cynicism* (Cambridge: Cambridge University Press, 2012).

16. Shea, *Cynic Enlightenment*, 132.

17. Shea, ix. This is discussed in more detail in note 3 of this chapter, drawing from the work of Niehues-Pröbsting, "The Modern Reception of Cynicism."

18. This is quoted from Stanley's gloss of Sloterdijk's argument regarding modern cynicism. See Sharon Stanley, "Retreat from Politics: The Cynic in Modern Times," *Polity* 39, no. 3 (2007): 385.

19. Shea, *Cynic Enlightenment*, 110.

20. Voltaire, cited in Mazella, *Making of Modern Cynicism*, 123.

21. Rousseau, cited in Niehues-Pröbsting, "Modern Reception of Cynicism," 342.

22. Mazella, *Making of Modern Cynicism*, 126.

23. Stanley argues that Rousseau cannot be considered a Cynic at all, at this stage, having severed all links with the "educational and missionary project" of the ancient Cynics in those last years, deciding to give up hope that he might change his fellow men (Stanley, *French Enlightenment and the Emergence of Modern Cynicism*, 153).

24. Mazella explores both interpretations and ultimately places his own somewhere in between, concluding that Rousseau is conflicted in his attempts at Cynic parrhesia, falling as such "far below Diogenes' ascetic standard" (Mazella, *Making of Modern Cynicism*, 138), and in some respects fully exemplifying the condition of "enlightened false consciousness" that Sloterdijk identifies in modern cynicism (Mazella, 136; Sloterdijk, *Critique of Cynical Reason*, 5).

25. Mazella, *Making of Modern Cynicism*, 117.

26. Mazella, 117.

27. In an ironic twist, however, as Rousseau's reputation fell to pieces he became a "potent partisan symbol of Enlightenment reason's historical failure" (Mazella, 142). He subsequently stood for the "danger of reason being perverted, reason turning into irrationality and madness, reason being frustrated because of its own far too exalted expectations" (Niehues-Pröbsting, "Modern Reception of Cynicism," 333).

28. Sloterdijk, *Critique of Cynical Reason*, 54.

29. Mazella, *Making of Modern Cynicism*, 116.

30. Mazella, 116.

31. Jean-Jacques Rousseau, *Emile, or On Education*, trans. A. Bloom (London: Penguin, 1991).

32. Sloterdijk, *Critique of Cynical Reason*, 56.

33. Here I paraphrase and adapt an argument from Sloterdijk (see *Critique of Cynical Reason*, 58). On the question of the benevolent violence of education more generally, see Allen, *Benign Violence*. On the refusal or inability of educators to doubt education in modernity, see Allen, "The End of Education." And on the mutually reinforcing operations of instrumental reason and atrophied ideals in educational settings, see Ansgar Allen and Roy Goddard, *Education and Philosophy: An Introduction* (London: Sage, 2017), 123.

34. Sloterdijk, *Critique of Cynical Reason*, 57.

35. Denis Diderot, "Rameau's Nephew," in *Rameau's Nephew and D'Alembert's Dream*, trans. Leonard Tancock (London: Penguin, 1966). As discussed by Shea, *Cynic Enlightenment*, and Stanley, *French Enlightenment and the Emergence of Modern Cynicism*; "The Cynic in Modern Times."

36. Stanley, *French Enlightenment and the Emergence of Modern Cynicism*, 136.

37. Shea, *Cynic Enlightenment*, 59.

38. Stanley, *French Enlightenment and the Emergence of Modern Cynicism*, 76.

39. Stanley, 138.

40. Stanley, 86 (emphasis mine).

41. Diderot, "Rameau's Nephew," 35.

42. Stanley, *French Enlightenment and the Emergence of Modern Cynicism*, 140.

43. Diderot, "Rameau's Nephew," 52.

44. Shea, *Cynic Enlightenment*, 111.

45. Marquis de Sade, *Philosophy in the Bedroom*, in *The Complete Justine, Philosophy in the Bedroom, and Other Writings*, trans. Richard Seaver and Austryn Wainhouse (New York: Grove Press, 1965).

46. Shea, *Cynic Enlightenment*, 111.

47. Allen, *Cynical Educator*, 137; Allen, "Education, Mastery and the Marquis de Sade," *Other Education: The Journal of Educational Alternatives* 5, no. 2 (2016).

48. Sade, *Philosophy in the Bedroom*, 185.

49. See, for example, the gargantuan *Juliette* (New York: Grove Press, 1968).

50. Shea, *Cynic Enlightenment*, 126.

51. The role of pleasure in Sade is, it should be noted, not as straightforward as it first appears (hence Sade only contorts rather than travesties Cynicism on this count), since the desire for pleasure must itself be eliminated by the libertine who wishes to become free of all entrapments; Sade's libertine is unusual, though, in that pleasure must be overcome by its exhaustion, by excessive experience of all varieties of pleasure, rather than by denial (see Allen, *Cynical Educator*, 142). In this respect, Sade appears close to the Cynic once more, practicing to excess what the Cynic seeks to transform. Perhaps a sharper distinction between Sadean libertinage and ancient Cynicism may be drawn by the extreme individualism of the former, which seeks, as its limit, to become entirely indifferent to all other human beings, beyond the reach of pity (Allen, 143).

52. Cavarero, *In Spite of Plato*, 55.

53. Allen, "Education, Mastery and the Marquis de Sade," 43.

54. See, for example, Julietta Singh, *Unthinking Mastery: Dehumanism and Decolonial Entanglements* (Durham, NC: Duke University Press, 2018).

55. See Jane Gallop, "The Immoral Teachers," *Yale French Studies* 63 (1982).

56. Simone de Beauvoir, "Must We Burn Sade?" in *The 120 Days of Sodom and Other Writings—Marquis de Sade*, ed. Austryn Wainhouse and Richard Seaver (New York: Grove Press, 1966), 21.

57. de Beauvoir, "Must We Burn Sade?," 29.

58. As Foucault characterizes it, "Sade formulated an eroticism proper to a disciplinary society: a regulated, anatomical, hierarchical society whose time is carefully distributed, its spaces partitioned, characterized by obedience and surveillance" (Michel Foucault, "Sade: Sergeant of Sex," in *Essential Works of Foucault 1954–1984*, volume 2, ed. James Faubion, trans. John Johnston [London: Penguin, 2000], 226).

59. Maurice Blanchot, *Lautréamont and Sade* (Stanford: Stanford University Press, 2004).

60. Allen, *Cynical Educator*, 147–148.

Chapter 7

1. Here and in what follows I draw from and refer the reader to Mazella, *Making of Modern Cynicism*, 143–162.

2. The list of recent complaints against cynicism is long. Here is an indicative selection: Donald L. Kanter and Philip H. Mirvis, *The Cynical Americans: Living and Working in an Age of Discontent and Disillusion* (San Francisco: Jossey-Bass, 1989); Jeffrey C. Goldfarb, *The Cynical Society: The Culture of Politics and the Politics of Culture in American Life* (Chicago: University of Chicago Press, 1991); Richard Stivers, *The Culture of Cynicism: American Morality in Decline* (Malden, MA: Blackwell, 1994); Michael Lerner, *The Politics of Meaning: Restoring Hope and Possibility in an Age of Cynicism* (New York: Perseus Books, 1997); Joseph N. Cappella and Kathleen Hall Jamieson, *Spiral of Cynicism: The Press and the Public Good* (Oxford: Oxford University Press, 1997); Ronald C. Arnett and Pat Arneson, *Dialogic Civility in a Cynical Age: Community, Hope, and Interpersonal Relationships* (Albany: SUNY Press, 1999); William Chaloupka, *Everybody Knows: Cynicism in America* (Minneapolis: University of Minnesota Press, 1999); Henry A. Giroux, *Public Spaces, Private Lives: Beyond the Culture of Cynicism* (Lanham, MD: Rowman & Littlefield, 2001); Susan Haack, *Defending Science—within Reason: Between Scientism and Cynicism* (New York: Prometheus Books, 2007); Wilber W. Caldwell, *Cynicism and the Evolution of the American Dream* (Washington: Potomac Books, 2007); Megan Mustain, *Overcoming Cynicism: William James and the Metaphysics of Engagement* (New York: Continuum, 2011); Stella C. Batagiannis, Barry Kanpol, and Anna V. Wilson, eds., *The Hope for Audacity: From Cynicism to Hope in Educational Leadership and Policy* (New York: Peter Lang, 2012); John Hagan, Joshua Kaiser, and Anna Hanson, *Iraq and the Crimes of Aggressive War: The Legal Cynicism of Criminal Militarism*, Cambridge Studies in Law and Society (Cambridge: Cambridge University Press, 2015).

3. The consequences of which are discussed (and bemoaned) in Lee McIntyre, *Post-Truth* (Cambridge, MA: MIT Press, 2018).

4. Caldwell, *Cynicism and the Evolution of the American Dream*.

5. Arnett and Arneson, *Dialogic Civility in a Cynical Age*.

6. Cappella and Jamieson, *Spiral of Cynicism*.

7. Giroux, *Public Spaces, Private Lives*.

8. Hagan, Kaiser, and Hanson, *Iraq and the Crimes of Aggressive War*.

9. Paolo Virno, *A Grammar of the Multitude* (Los Angeles: Semiotext[e], 2004), 88.

10. J. D. Taylor, *Negative Capitalism: Cynicism in the Neoliberal Era* (Winchester: Zero, 2013), 33.

11. Taylor, *Negative Capitalism*, 32.

12. Theodor Adorno, "Theses Against Occultism," in *The Stars Down to Earth and Other Essays on the Irrational in Culture*, ed. Stephen Crook (London: Routledge, 2002), 174. Elsewhere, Adorno writes: "Cynical soberness is probably more characteristic of the fascist mentality than psychological intoxication" ("Anti-Semitism and Fascist Propaganda," in *Stars Down to Earth*, 222).

13. Taylor, *Negative Capitalism*, 103.

14. Timothy Bewes, *Cynicism and Postmodernity* (London: Verso, 1997), 26.

15. Bewes, *Cynicism and* Postmodernity, 26.

16. Terry Eagleton, *Ideology: An Introduction* (London: Verso, 2007), 38.

17. Jürgen Habermas, *The Philosophical Discourse of Modernity*, trans. Frederick Lawrence (Cambridge: Polity, 1985), 253. Against this position, I would claim that although many post-Foucauldian writers might be taken to task for their cynicisms (in the modern, debased sense of the word), that is to say, for justifying why they must abandon radical collective action, Foucault's politics are less obviously cynical in this sense. See Ansgar Allen and Roy Goddard, "The Domestication of Foucault: Government, Critique, War," *History of the Human Sciences* 27, no. 5 (2014).

18. Bewes, *Cynicism and Postmodernity*, 6–8.

19. Alexei Yurchak, "The Cynical Reason of Late Socialism: Power, Pretense, and the Anekdot," *Public Culture* 9, no. 2 (1997); *Everything Was Forever, Until It Was No More: The Last Soviet Generation* (Princeton: Princeton University Press, 2005); Mark Lipovetsky, *Charms of the Cynical Reason: The Trickster's Transformations in Soviet and Post-Soviet Culture* (Boston: Academic Studies Press, 2011); Hans Steinmüller and Susanne Brandtstädter, eds., *Irony, Cynicism and the Chinese State* (London: Routledge, 2016).

20. Stanley, *French Enlightenment and the Emergence of Modern Cynicism*.

21. Mazella, *Making of Modern Cynicism*; Shea, *Cynic Enlightenment*; Stanley, *French Enlightenment and the Emergence of Modern Cynicism*.

22. Yurchak, "Cynical Reason of Late Socialism." For an expanded version of his argument, see *Everything Was Forever*.

23. Yurchak, "Cynical Reason of Late Socialism," 185.

24. Yurchak, 163.

25. Yurchak, 185.

26. Yurchak, 186.

27. For a notable exception, see Shea, *Cynic Enlightenment*, 146–168.

28. Sloterdijk, *Critique of Cynical Reason*, 5.

29. Hannah Arendt, "Introduction: Walter Benjamin 1892–1940," in *Illuminations* (London: Pimlico, 1999), 14.

30. For a rare example in which Sloterdijk's call to impudence is taken seriously and endorsed, see Chaloupka, *Everybody Knows*. See also the discussion in Shea, *Cynic Enlightenment*.

31. Sloterdijk, *Critique of Cynical Reason*, 5.

32. Sloterdijk, 379.

33. This can be distinguished from the humour of *anekdoty* that Yurchak writes about. Yurchak describes a form of cynical humor that "differs from both jaded cynicism and explicit acts of kynic [Cynic] ridicule and subversion of dominant norms, and refuses to be charged with the moral pathos of exposing 'lies' and stating 'truths'" (Yurchak, *Everything Was Forever*, 277).

34. Shea, *Cynic Enlightenment*, 155.

35. Mazella, *Making of Modern Cynicism*, 224.

36. Slavoj Žižek, *The Sublime Object of Ideology* (London: Verso, 2008), 27.

37. As Žižek argues, ideology now functions in such a way that it can "afford to reveal the secret of its functioning ... *without in the least affecting its efficiency*" (*The Indivisible Remainder: On Schelling and Related Matters* [London: Verso, 2007]).

38. To paraphrase Sloterdijk, *Critique of Cynical Reason*, 5.

39. Mazella inclines in this direction, but the argument is made most forcefully by Stanley, *French Enlightenment and the Emergence of Modern Cynicism*. See also Ian Cutler, "The Cynical Manager," *Management Learning* 31, no. 2 (2000); Christopher J. Gilbert, "In Dubiis Libertas: A Diogenic Attitude for a Politics of Distrust," *Rhetoric Society Quarterly* 42, no. 1 (2012); Arthur Rose, Robbie Duschinsky, and Jane Macnaughton, "Cynicism as a Strategic Virtue," *Lancet* 389, no. 10070 (2017). For a rare exception in which a stronger, more confrontational cynicism is advocated, in this case to "reopen old wounds, to take up conversations about 'enhanced interrogation' that petered out much too soon," to raise the scandalous, scandalizing suggestion that all US citizens should see themselves as somehow complicit in the government-sanctioned use of torture by the US military at Abu Ghraib, see Laura Sparks, "Re-seeing Abu Ghraib: Cynical Rhetoric as Civic Engagement," *Present Tense: A Journal of Rhetoric in Society* 5, no. 3 (2016): 6.

40. Stanley, *French Enlightenment and the Emergence of Modern Cynicism*, 21.

41. Stanley, 181.

42. Mazella, *Making of Modern Cynicism*, 171.

43. Nietzsche, *Ecce Homo*, 43.

44. See note 22 in chapter 3.

45. Friedrich Nietzsche, *The Birth of Tragedy: Out of the Spirit of Music*, trans. S. Whiteside (London: Penguin, 2003), "Attempt at Self-Criticism," §1.

46. Niehues-Pröbsting, "Modern Reception of Cynicism," 353–363.

47. That Nietzsche was aware of this anecdote is clear from his earlier work, where he mentions it explicitly: "Before one seeks men one must have found the lantern. Will it have to be the lantern of the Cynic?" (Friedrich Nietzsche, "The Wanderer and His Shadow," in *Human, All Too Human*, trans. R. J. Hollingdale [Cambridge: Cambridge University Press, 1996], §18).

48. Laertius, *Lives of Eminent Philosophers*, 6.41.

49. Friedrich Nietzsche, *The Gay Science: With a Prelude in Rhymes and an Appendix of Songs*, trans. W. Kaufmann (New York: Vintage, 1974), §125. If Nietzsche's madman represents the Cynic in this passage, as he appears to, it is significant that he fails in this very different historical context to stir those about him into reflecting on their condition. Indeed, the very lantern that evokes the Cynic episode is thrown to the ground so that it breaks into pieces and expires.

50. Martin Heidegger, "Nietzsche's Word: 'God Is Dead,'" in *Off the Beaten Track*, ed. Julian Young and Kenneth Haynes, trans. J. Young and K. Haynes (Cambridge: Cambridge University Press, 2002), 160.

51. Hunter, *Rethinking the School*, xxi.

52. Kant's famous definition in full: "Enlightenment is man's release from his self-incurred tutelage. Tutelage is the incapacity to use one's own understanding without the guidance of another. Such tutelage is self-imposed if its cause is not lack of intelligence, but rather a lack of determination and courage to use one's intelligence without being guided by another." Self-incurred tutelage has also been translated as "self-incurred immaturity." See Immanuel Kant, "An Answer to the Question: What Is Enlightenment?" in *What Is Enlightenment: Eighteenth-Century Answers and Twentieth-Century Questions*, ed. J. Schmidt (Berkeley: University of California Press, 1996), 58. This might be a more accurate translation, though "tutelage" has the advantage of emphasizing how immaturity is used to justify subordination to education, understood as a form of both guardianship and instruction. The irony is that Kant's motto of enlightenment, "*Sapere aude!* Have the courage to use your *own* understanding" (58), helps justify the huge expansion of modern education once societies travel out of the prior phase of "self-incurred immaturity." Education becomes the inalienable right of all, and thereby operates as a system of

universal guardianship and instruction far more extensive in reach and extent than "immature" societies ever dreamed.

53. Mark A. Wrathall, *Heidegger and Unconcealment: Truth, Language and History* (Cambridge: Cambridge University Press, 2011), 198.

54. Friedrich Nietzsche, *The Will to Power*, trans. W. Kaufman and R. J. Hollingdale (New York: Vintage, 1968), §585.

55. Nietzsche, *Gay Science*, §125.

56. Sigmund Freud, "Mourning and Melancholia," in *The Standard Edition of the Complete Psychological Works of Sigmund Freud*, volume 14, ed. James Strachey (London: Vintage, 2001).

57. Freud, "Mourning and Melancholia," 245.

58. For a discussion of how this manifests in the figure of the melancholic educator, see Allen, *Cynical Educator*, 89–90.

59. This might seem a departure from Freud, yet the melancholic cynic has not yet generally risen to the pitch of frustration and lament Freud describes in his clinical discussion (Sloterdijk describes today's cynics as "borderline melancholics," *Critique of Cynical Reason*, 5), that is to say, the modern cynic has not yet reached the level of despair that might propel the sufferer to Freud's waiting room in search of a cure.

60. Luis Navia, *Diogenes of Sinope: The Man in the Tub* (Westport, CT: Greenwood Press, 1998), 147.

61. Nietzsche, "Anti-Christ," §23.

62. Gianni Vattimo, *The End of Modernity: Nihilism and Hermeneutics in Postmodern Culture* (Cambridge: Polity, 2002), 169.

63. Nietzsche cited in Niehues-Pröbsting, "Modern Reception of Cynicism," 359. A slightly different translation will be found in Friedrich Nietzsche, *Beyond Good and Evil: Prelude to a Philosophy of the Future*, trans. Marion Faber (Oxford: Oxford University Press, 1998), §26.

64. Sloterdijk, *Critique of Cynical Reason*, xxvi.

65. Sloterdijk, xxvi.

66. Sloterdijk, xxix.

67. For reasons outlined in Allen, "End of Education."

68. Sloterdijk, *Critique of Cynical Reason*, xxix.

69. See Kevin Flint and Nick Peim, *Rethinking the Education Improvement Agenda: A Critical Philosophical Approach* (London: Continuum, 2012).

70. See Kenneth Wain, "The Learning Society: Postmodern Politics," *International Journal of Lifelong Education* 19, no. 1 (2000).

71. Sloterdijk, *Critique of Cynical Reason*, xxxii.

72. Sloterdijk, 5.

73. Sloterdijk, 5.

74. Sloterdijk, 154.

75. Sloterdijk, 151.

76. Sloterdijk, 151 (my emphasis).

77. Dominique Laporte, *History of Shit*, trans. Nadia Benabid and Rodolphe el-Khoury (Cambridge, MA: MIT Press, 2002), 63.

Chapter 8

1. Rebecca Higgie, "Kynical Dogs and Cynical Masters: Contemporary Satire, Politics and Truth-Telling," *Humor* 27, no. 2 (2014).

2. Lipovetsky, *Charms of the Cynical Reason*. The link between the trickster and the Cynic has even used to build an interpretive frame for understanding non-Western dissemblers; such as the figure of Wakdjunkaga who, in Native American folklore, breaks "every possible taboo" and creates "havoc by not being able to control his sphincter muscle" (Klaus-Peter Koepping, "Absurdity and Hidden Truth: Cunning Intelligence and Grotesque Body Images as Manifestations of the Trickster," *History of Religions* 24, no. 3 [1985]: 207). See also Paul Radin, *The Trickster: A Study in American Indian Mythology* (New York: Schocken Books, 1972).

3. Gilbert, "In Dubiis Libertas."

4. Mark Lipovetsky, "Pussy Riot as the Trickstar," *Apparatus. Film, Media and Digital Cultures in Central and Eastern Europe* 1 (2015); Peter Osborne, "Disguised as a Dog," *Radical Philosophy* 174 (July–August 2012); Annika Skoglund and Johannes Stripple, "From Climate Skeptic to Climate Cynic," *Critical Policy Studies* (2018). It has been suggested to me that one might add the Yes Men to this list—two culture-jamming activists who gained some notoriety in the first decade of the twenty-first century with a series of pranks directed at George W. Bush, the World Trade Organization, and global multinational power. The Yes Men (in particular their 2003 film by the same name) might be understood through a Cynic framework, insofar as they overidentify with, exaggerate, and thereby lampoon the logic of global capital. This bears analogy to the Cynic commitment to live a "sovereign" existence, in which the Cynic took that idea—by which other non-Cynic philosophers distinguished themselves—to its radical endpoint, an expression of "sovereignty" that its non-Cynic practitioners and advocates would find abhorrent. The idea was to exaggerate a commitment to the point of absurdity. The Yes Men do not achieve such results, however. Their analysis of globalization offers little to surprise left-wing critics (Michael Moore appears in the first film simply to endorse their analysis). It also fails to upset its advocates and lackeys, as can

be seen by the audience reaction to their gold spandex body suit spoof, with its rectal sensors and worker monitoring screen attached to a huge inflatable phallus. The audience is mildly amused, and not appalled. In other stunts, when an audience is sufficiently disturbed—by the idea of recycling "first world" human sewage for consumption by "third world" customers—their disgust is expressed within an entirely predictable evaluative framework that is not itself perturbed by the format of the prank.

5. Shaun Walker, "Petr Pavlensky: Why I Nailed My Scrotum to Red Square," *Guardian*, February 5, 2014.

6. Marc Bennetts, "Acts of Resistance: Pyotr Pavlensky on Performance Art as Protest," *Calvert Journal*, December 1, 2014.

7. Bennetts, "Acts of Resistance."

8. Bennetts, "Acts of Resistance."

9. Walker, "Petr Pavlensky."

10. Bennetts, "Acts of Resistance."

11. Tatyana Dvornikova, "'We refused Everything France Wanted to Give Us': Oksana Shalygina's First Post-Prison Interview," *openDemocracy*, January 25, 2018.

12. See Benjamin Schreier, *The Power of Negative Thinking: Cynicism and the History of Modern American Literature* (Charlottesville: University of Virginia Press, 2009); Mark Sussman, "Cynicism and *The Damnation of Theron Ware*," *Novel: A Forum on Fiction* 47, no. 3 (2014); Kieran Curran, *Cynicism in British Post-War Culture: Ignorance, Dust and Disease* (Basingstoke: Palgrave Macmillan, 2015); Arthur Rose, *Literary Cynics: Borges, Beckett, Coetzee* (London: Bloomsbury, 2017).

13. William Desmond, *Cynics* (Stocksfield: Acumen, 2008), 209.

14. For instance, Rose "subtracts" his own conception of cynicism from this broad and sprawling field. In the late style of Jorge Luis Borges, Samuel Beckett, and J. M. Coetzee, Rose detects a "literary cynicism," defined as a species of cynicism that submits its own style and claim to authority to cynic critique (Rose, *Literary Cynics*).

15. This has been attempted, but the results were mixed. See Mechtild Widrich, "The Informative Public of Performance: A Study of Viennese Actionism, 1965–1970," *Drama Review* 57, no. 1 (2013); Allen, *Cynical Educator*, 192.

16. Mazella, *Making of Modern Cynicism*, 27.

17. Sloterdijk, *Critique of Cynical Reason*, 164.

18. Jarett Kobek, *I Hate the Internet* (Los Angeles: We Heard You Like Books, 2016), 3.

19. Sloterdijk, *Critique of Cynical Reason*, 194 (emphasis in original). In what follows I draw from and in some places extend arguments made in Allen, *Cynical Educator*.

20. Luc Boltanski and Eve Chiapello, *The New Spirit of Capitalism* (London: Verso, 2007); Luc Boltanski, "The Left after May 1968 and the Longing for Total Revolution," *Thesis Eleven* 69 (2002).

21. Carl Cederström and Peter Fleming, *Dead Man Working* (Winchester: Zero Books, 2011).

22. Michael E. Gardiner, "The Grandchildren of Marx and Coca-Cola: Lefebvre, Utopia and the 'Recuperation' of Everyday Life," in *Globalization and Utopia: Critical Essays*, ed. Patrick Hayden and Chamsy El-Ojeili (Basingstoke: Palgrave Macmillan, 2009), 228.

23. Mark Fisher, *Capitalist Realism: Is There No Alternative?* (Ropley: Zero Books, 2009), 15.

24. Slavoj Žižek, *The Metastases of Enjoyment: Six Essays on Women and Causality* (London: Verso, 2005). For an analysis of how this repressive function might be modeled in an educational environment, see Clarke's analysis of Keating's role, as transgressive/oppressive teacher in the film *Dead Poet's Society*: Matthew Clarke, "Education beyond Reason and Redemption: A Detour through the Death Drive," *Pedagogy, Culture & Society* (2019).

25. Foucault, *Courage of Truth*, 263.

26. Foucault, 262.

27. Foucault, 262.

28. See Michel Foucault, *The Birth of Biopolitics: Lectures at the Collège de France 1978–1979* (Basingstoke: Palgrave Macmillan, 2008). For a worked-out example, see my argument about the relationship between the birth of statistics and eugenics in the nineteenth century, and the development of meritocracy in the twentieth, in Allen, *Benign Violence*.

29. As discussed in Hadot, *Philosophy as a Way of Life*.

30. Leo Bersani, *Homos* (Cambridge, MA: Harvard University Press, 1995); Robert McRuer, *Crip Theory: Cultural Signs of Queerness and Disability* (New York: NYU Press, 2006); Lee Edelman, *No Future: Queer Theory and the Death Drive* (Durham, NC: Duke University Press, 2004). Though in relation to the first two, the Cynic does not resource him- or herself on (i) the idea that an appreciation of the challenge posed by nonnormative bodies will shake fixed conceptions of human possibility and thereby facilitate an expanded and less harmful conception of the human; or (ii) the hope that the pursuit of transgressive sexuality will reorganize our frameworks of desire and inaugurate a

less manipulative, more ethical relation to the other. These arguments are worth engaging, but they do not *ground* Cynic transgression.

31. This question has been described as "the Sphinx of the left" since it sets in play a riddle most fail to resolve as they retreat into moralistic rejection, or worse, a sympathetic paternalism that "understands" the riot as the unconscious acting out of the injustices of global capital. See Jasper Bernes and Joshua Clover, "History and the Sphinx: Of Riots and Uprisings," *Los Angeles Review of Books*, September 24, 2012.

32. Yurchak, "Cynical Reason of Late Socialism."

33. Yurchak, 161.

BIBLIOGRAPHY

Adorno, Theodor. "Anti-Semitism and Fascist Propaganda." In *The Stars Down to Earth and Other Essays on the Irrational in Culture*, edited by Stephen Crook. London: Routledge, 2002. Originally published 1946.

Adorno, Theodor. "Theses against Occultism." In *The Stars Down to Earth and Other Essays on the Irrational in Culture*, edited by Stephen Crook. London: Routledge, 2002. Originally published 1947.

Allen, Ansgar. "Awaiting Education: Friedrich Nietzsche on the Future of Our Educational Institutions." *Philosophical Inquiry in Education* 24, no. 2 (2017): 197–210.

Allen, Ansgar. *Benign Violence: Education in and beyond the Age of Reason*. Basingstoke: Palgrave Macmillan, 2014.

Allen, Ansgar. *The Cynical Educator*. Leicester: Mayfly, 2017.

Allen, Ansgar. "Education, Mastery and the Marquis de Sade." *Other Education: The Journal of Educational Alternatives* 5, no. 2 (2016): 39–55.

Allen, Ansgar. "The End of Education: Nietzsche, Foucault, Genealogy." *Philosophical Inquiry in Education* 25, no. 1 (2018): 47–65.

Allen, Ansgar, and Roy Goddard. "The Domestication of Foucault: Government, Critique, War." *History of the Human Sciences* 27, no. 5 (2014): 26–53.

Allen, Ansgar, and Roy Goddard. *Education and Philosophy: An Introduction*. London: Sage, 2017.

Arendt, Hannah. "Introduction: Walter Benjamin 1892–1940." In *Illuminations*. London: Pimlico, 1999. Originally published 1970.

Armstrong, Deann. "Hanging the Watch: Erotic Timekeeping and Temporal Cynicism in *The Roaring Girl*." *Modern Philology* 116, no. 2 (2018): 145–163.

Arnett, Ronald C., and Pat Arneson. *Dialogic Civility in a Cynical Age: Community, Hope, and Interpersonal Relationships*. Albany: SUNY Press, 1999.

Augustine. *Concerning the City of God against the Pagans*. Translated by Henry Bettenson. London: Penguin, 2003.

Bakhtin, Mikhail. *The Dialogic Imagination: Four Essays*. Translated by Caryl Emerson and Michael Holquist. Austin: University of Texas Press, 1981.

Bakhtin, Mikhail. *Rabelais and His World*. Translated by Helene Iswolsky. Bloomington: Indiana University Press, 1984.

Batagiannis, Stella C., Barry Kanpol, and Anna V. Wilson, eds. *The Hope for Audacity: From Cynicism to Hope in Educational Leadership and Policy*. New York: Peter Lang, 2012.

Beauvoir, Simone de. "Must We Burn Sade?" In *The 120 Days of Sodom and Other Writings—Marquis de Sade*, edited by Austryn Wainhouse and Richard Seaver. New York: Grove Press, 1966. Originally published 1951.

Bennetts, Marc. "Acts of Resistance: Pyotr Pavlensky on Performance Art as Protest." *Calvert Journal*, December 1, 2014.

Bernes, Jasper, and Joshua Clover. "History and the Sphinx: Of Riots and Uprisings." *Los Angeles Review of Books*, September 24, 2012.

Bersani, Leo. *Homos*. Cambridge, MA: Harvard University Press, 1995.

Betz, Hans Dieter. "Jesus and the Cynics: Survey and Analysis of a Hypothesis." *Journal of Religion* 74, no. 4 (1994): 453–475.

Bewes, Timothy. *Cynicism and Postmodernity*. London: Verso, 1997.

Billerbeck, Margarethe. "The Ideal Cynic from Epictetus to Julian." In *The Cynics: The Cynic Movement in Antiquity and Its Legacy*, edited by R. Bracht Branham and Marie-Odile Goulet-Gazé. Berkeley: University of California Press, 1996.

Blanchot, Maurice. *Lautréamont and Sade*. Stanford: Stanford University Press, 2004. Originally published 1949.

Boltanski, Luc. "The Left after May 1968 and the Longing for Total Revolution." *Thesis Eleven* 69, no. 1 (2002): 1–20.

Boltanski, Luc, and Eve Chiapello. *The New Spirit of Capitalism*. London: Verso, 2007. Originally published in French in 1999.

Bracht Branham, R. "Defacing the Currency: Diogenes' Rhetoric and the *Invention* of Cynicism." In *The Cynics: The Cynic Movement in Antiquity and Its Legacy*, edited by R. Bracht Branham and Marie-Odile Goulet-Gazé. Berkeley: University of California Press, 1996.

Bracht Branham, R. "Introduction." In *The Cynics: The Cynic Movement in Antiquity and Its Legacy*, edited by R. Bracht Branham and Marie-Odile Goulet-Gazé. Berkeley: University of California Press, 1996.

Bracht Branham, R. "Nietzsche's Cynicism: Uppercase or lowercase?" In *Nietzsche and Antiquity*, edited by Paul Bishop. New York: Camden House, 2004.

Bracht Branham, R. *Unruly Eloquence: Lucian and the Comedy of Traditions*. Cambridge, MA: Harvard University Press, 1989.

Bracht Branham, R., and Marie-Odile Goulet-Gazé, eds. *The Cynics: The Cynic Movement in Antiquity and Its Legacy*. Berkeley: University of California Press, 1996.

Brown, Peter. *Power and Persuasion in Late Antiquity: Towards a Christian Empire*. Madison: University of Wisconsin Press, 1992.

Caldwell, Wilber W. *Cynicism and the Evolution of the American Dream*. Washington, DC: Potomac Books, 2007.

Cappella, Joseph N., and Kathleen Hall Jamieson. *Spiral of Cynicism: The Press and the Public Good*. Oxford: Oxford University Press, 1997.

Caputi, Anthony. *John Marston, Satirist*. Ithaca, NY: Cornell University Press, 1961.

Cavarero, Adriana. *In Spite of Plato: A Feminist Rewriting of Ancient Philosophy*. Cambridge: Polity, 1995.

Cederström, Carl, and Peter Fleming. *Dead Man Working*. Winchester: Zero Books, 2011.

Chaloupka, William. *Everybody Knows: Cynicism in America*. Minneapolis: University of Minnesota Press, 1999.

Clarke, Matthew. "Education beyond Reason and Redemption: A Detour through the Death Drive." *Pedagogy, Culture & Society* 27, no. 2 (2019): 183–197.

Clay, Diskin. *Lucian of Samosata: Four Philosophical Lives (Nigrinus, Demonax, Peregrinus, Alexander Pseudomantis)*. Edited by Wolfgang Haase. Berlin: Walter de Gruyter, 1992.

Clément, Michéle. *Le Cynisme à la Renaissance d'Érasme à Montaigne*. Geneva: Droz, 2005.

Cooper, John M. *Pursuits of Wisdom: Six Ways of Life in Ancient Philosophy from Socrates to Plotinus*. Princeton, NJ: Princeton University Press, 2012.

Corrington, Gail Paterson. "The Defense of the Body and the Discourse of Appetite: Continence and Control in the Greco-Roman World." *Semeia* 57 (1992): 65–74.

Crossan, John Dominic. *The Historical Jesus: The Life of a Mediterranean Jewish Peasant*. New York: Harper Collins, 1992.

Curran, Kieran. *Cynicism in British Post-War Culture: Ignorance, Dust and Disease*. Basingstoke: Palgrave Macmillan, 2015.

Cutler, Ian. "The Cynical Manager." *Management Learning* 31, no. 2 (2000): 295–312.

Cutler, Ian. *Cynicism from Diogenes to Dilbert*. Jefferson, NC: McFarland, 2005.

Delbanco, Andrew. *College: What It Was, Is, and Should Be*. Princeton: Princeton University Press, 2011.

Deresiewicz, William. *Excellent Sheep: The Miseducation of the American Elite and the Way to a Meaningful Life*. New York: The Free Press, 2014.

Déroche, Vincent. *Études sur Léontios de Néapolis*. Upsalla: Upsalla Universitet, 1995.

Desmond, William. *Cynics*. Stocksfield: Acumen, 2008.

Detienne, Marcel, and Jean-Pierre Vernant. *Cunning Intelligence in Greek Culture and Society*. Translated by Janet Lloyd. Hassocks: Harvester Press, 1978.

Diderot, Denis. "Rameau's Nephew." Translated by Leonard Tancock. In *Rameau's Nephew and D'Alembert's Dream*. London: Penguin, 1966.

Diogenes. *Diogenes the Cynic: Sayings and Anecdotes*. Oxford: Oxford University Press, 2012.

Doeuff, Michèle Le. *Hipparchia's Choice: An Essay Concerning Women, Philosophy, Etc*. New York: Columbia University Press, 2007. Originally published in French, 1989.

Downing, F. Gerald. *Christ and the Cynics: Jesus and other Radical Preachers in First-Century Tradition*. Sheffield: Sheffield Academic Press, 1988.

Downing, F. Gerald. *Cynics, Paul and the Pauline Churches*. London: Routledge, 1998.

Downing, F. Gerald. *Cynics and Christian Origins*. Edinburgh: T&T Clark, 1992.

Downing, F. Gerald. "Deeper Reflections on the Jewish Cynic Jesus." *Journal of Biblical Literature* 117, no. 1 (1998): 97–104.

Dudley, Donald R. *A History of Cynicism: From Diogenes to the 6th Century AD*. London: Methuen, 1937.

Duval, Edwin M. *The Design of Rabelais's Tiers Livre de Pantagruel*. Geneva: Droz, 1997.

Dvornikova, Tatyana. "'We Refused Everything France Wanted to Give Us': Oksana Shalygina's First Post-Prison Interview." *openDemocracy*, January 25, 2018.

Eagleton, Terry. *Ideology: An Introduction*. London: Verso, 2007.

Eagleton, Terry. "The Subject of Literature." *Cultural Critique* 2 (1985): 95–104.

Eddy, Paul Rhodes. "Jesus as Diogenes? Reflections on the Cynic Jesus Thesis." *Journal of Biblical Literature* 115, no. 3 (1996): 449–469.

Edelman, Lee. *No Future: Queer Theory and the Death Drive*. Durham, NC: Duke University Press, 2004.

Edmundson, Mark. *Why Teach? In Defense of a Real Education*. New York: Bloomsbury, 2013.

Epictetus. "On Cynicism (Discourse 3.22)." Translated by R. Dobbin. In *The Cynic Philosophers from Diogenes to Julian*, edited by Robert Dobbin. London: Penguin, 2012.

Fisher, Mark. *Capitalist Realism: Is There No Alternative?* Ropley: Zero Books, 2009.

Flint, Kevin, and Nick Peim. *Rethinking the Education Improvement Agenda: A Critical Philosophical Approach*. London: Continuum, 2012.

Flynn, Thomas. "Foucault as Parrhesiast: His Last Course at the Collège de France (1984)." In *The Final Foucault*, edited by James Bernauer and David Rasmussen. Cambridge, MA: MIT Press, 1987.

Foucault, Michel. *The Birth of Biopolitics: Lectures at the Collège de France 1978–1979*. Basingstoke: Palgrave Macmillan, 2008. Originally published in French, 1979.

Foucault, Michel. *The Courage of Truth: Lectures at the Collège de France 1983–1984*. Translated by G. Burchell. Basingstoke: Palgrave Macmillan, 2011. Originally published in French, 1984.

Foucault, Michel. *Fearless Speech*. Los Angeles: Semiotext(e), 2001.

Foucault, Michel. *The Hermeneutics of the Subject: Lectures at the Collège de France 1981–1982*. Translated by G. Burchell. Basingstoke: Palgrave Macmillan, 2005. Originally published in French, 1982.

Foucault, Michel. "Sade: Sergeant of Sex." Translated by John Johnston. In *Essential Works of Foucault 1954–1984*, volume 2, edited by James Faubion. London: Penguin, 2000. Originally published in French, 1975.

Foucault, Michel. *The Will to Knowledge*. Translated by Robert Hurley. London: Penguin, 1998. Originally published in French, 1976.

Freud, Sigmund. "Civilization and Its Discontents." Translated by J. Strachey. In *The Standard Edition of the Complete Psychological Works of Sigmund Freud*, volume 21, edited by James Strachey. London: Vintage, 2001. Originally published 1930.

Freud, Sigmund. "Mourning and Melancholia." In *The Standard Edition of the Complete Psychological Works of Sigmund Freud*, volume 14, edited by James Strachey. London: Vintage, 2001. Originally published 1917.

Galen. *On the Passions and Errors of the Soul*. Columbus: Ohio State University Press, 1963.

Gallop, Jane. "The Immoral Teachers." *Yale French Studies* 63 (1982): 117–128.

Gardiner, Michael E. "The Grandchildren of Marx and Coca-Cola: Lefebvre, Utopia and the 'Recuperation' of Everyday Life." In *Globalization and Utopia: Critical Essays*, edited by Patrick Hayden and Chamsy El-Ojeili. Basingstoke: Palgrave Macmillan, 2009.

Gilbert, Christopher J. "In Dubiis Libertas: A Diogenic Attitude for a Politics of Distrust." *Rhetoric Society Quarterly* 42, no. 1 (2012).

Giroux, Henry A. *Public Spaces, Private Lives: Beyond the Culture of Cynicism*. Lanham, MD: Rowman & Littlefield, 2001.

Goldfarb, Jeffrey C. *The Cynical Society: The Culture of Politics and the Politics of Culture in American Life*. Chicago: University of Chicago Press, 1991.

Grafton, Anthony, and Lisa Jardine. *From Humanism to the Humanities: Education and the Liberal Arts in Fifteenth and Sixteenth-Century Europe*. London: Duckworth, 1986.

Haack, Susan. *Defending Science—within Reason: Between Scientism and Cynicism*. New York: Prometheus Books, 2007.

Habermas, Jürgen. *The Philosophical Discourse of Modernity*. Translated by Frederck Lawrence. Cambridge: Polity Press, 1985 [1987].

Hadot, Pierre. *Philosophy as a Way of Life*. Translated by Michael Chase. Oxford: Blackwell, 1995.

Hadot, Pierre. *What Is Ancient Philosophy?* Translated by Michael Chase. Cambridge, MA: Harvard University Press, 2004.

Hagan, John, Joshua Kaiser, and Anna Hanson. *Iraq and the Crimes of Aggressive War: The Legal Cynicism of Criminal Militarism*. Cambridge Studies in Law and Society. Cambridge: Cambridge University Press, 2015.

Heidegger, Martin. "Nietzsche's Word: 'God Is Dead.'" Translated by J. Young and K. Haynes. In *Off the Beaten Track*, edited by Julian Young and Kenneth Haynes. Cambridge: Cambridge University Press, 2002. Originally published in German, 1943.

Hershinow, David. "Cash Is King: Timon, Diogenes, and the Search for Sovereign Freedom." *Modern Philology* 115, no. 1 (2017): 53–79.

Hershinow, David. "Diogenes the Cynic and Shakespeare's Bitter Fool: The Politics and Aesthetics of Free Speech." *Criticism* 56, no. 4 (2014): 807–835.

Higgie, Rebecca. "Kynical Dogs and Cynical Masters: Contemporary Satire, Politics and Truth-Telling." *Humor* 27, no. 2 (2014): 183–201.

Honderich, Ted, ed. *The Oxford Companion to Philosophy*. 2nd edition. Oxford: Oxford University Press, 2005.

Hunter, Ian. *Culture and Government: The Emergence of Literary Education*. London: Macmillan, 1988.

Hunter, Ian. *Rethinking the School: Subjectivity, Bureaucracy, Criticism*. New York: St. Martin's Press, 1994.

Ingram, R. W. *John Marston*. Boston: Twayne Publishers, 1978.

Ivantov, Sergey A. *Holy Fools in Byzantium and Beyond*. Oxford: Oxford University Press, 2006.

Julian. "Against the Ignorant Cynics." Translated by R. Dobbin. In *The Cynic Philosophers from Diogenes to Julian*, edited by Robert Dobbin. London: Penguin, 2012.

Julian. "To the Cynic Heracleios." Translated by R. Dobbin. In *The Cynic Philosophers from Diogenes to Julian*, edited by Robert Dobbin. London: Penguin, 2012.

Julian. "To the Cynic Heracleios." Translated by W. C. Wright. In *The Works of the Emperor Julian*, volume 2, edited by Jeffrey Henderson. Loeb Classical Library. Cambridge, MA: Harvard University Press, 1913.

Julian. "To the Uneducated Cynics." Translated by W. C. Wright. In *The Works of the Emperor Julian*, volume 2, edited by Jeffrey Henderson. Loeb Classical Library. Cambridge, MA: Harvard University Press, 1913.

Kant, Immanuel. "An Answer to the Question: What Is Enlightenment?" In *What Is Enlightenment: Eighteenth-Century Answers and Twentieth-Century Questions*, edited by J. Schmidt. Berkeley: University of California Press, 1996. Originally published 1784.

Kanter, Donald L., and Philip H. Mirvis. *The Cynical Americans: Living and Working in an Age of Discontent and Disillusion*. San Francisco: Jossey-Bass, 1989.

Keenan, Alan. "Twilight of the Political? A Contribution to the Democratic Critique of Cynicism." *Theory & Event* 2, no. 1 (1998).

Kennedy, Kristen. "Cynic Rhetoric: The Ethics and Tactics of Resistance." *Rhetoric Review* 18, no. 1 (1999): 26–45.

Kennedy, Kristen. "Hipparchia the Cynic: Feminist Rhetoric and the Ethics of Embodiment." *Hypatia* 14, no. 2 (1999): 48–71.

Kersey, Ethel M. *Women Philosophers: A Biocritical Sourcebook*. New York: Greenwood Press, 1989.

Knights, Ben. *The Idea of the Clerisy in the Nineteenth Century*. Cambridge: Cambridge University Press, 1978.

Kobek, Jarett. *I Hate the Internet*. Los Angeles: We Heard You Like Books, 2016.

Koepping, Klaus-Peter. "Absurdity and Hidden Truth: Cunning Intelligence and Grotesque Body Images as Manifestations of the Trickster." *History of Religions* 24, no. 3 (1985): 191–214.

Krueger, Derek. "The Bawdy and Society: The Shamelessness of Diogenes in Roman Imperial Culture." In *The Cynics: The Cynic Movement in Antiquity and Its Legacy*, edited by R. Bracht Branham and Marie-Odile Goulet-Gazé. Berkeley: University of California Press, 1996.

Krueger, Derek. "Diogenes the Cynic among the Fourth Century Fathers." *Vigiliae Christianae* 47, no. 1 (1993): 29–49.

Krueger, Derek. *Symeon the Holy Fool: Leontius's Life and the Late Antique City*. Berkeley: University of California Press, 1996.

Ladkin, Sam, Robert McKay, and Emile Bojesen, eds. *Against Value in the Arts and Education*. London: Rowman & Littlefield, 2016.

Laertius, Diogenes. *Lives of Eminent Philosophers*, volume 2. Translated by R. D. Hicks. Edited by Jeffrey Henderson. Loeb Classical Library. Cambridge, MA: Harvard University Press, 1931.

Lang, Bernhard. "Jesus among the Philosophers: The Cynic Connection Explored and Affirmed, with a Note on Philo's Jewish-Cynic Philosophy." In *Religio-Philosophical Discourses in the Mediterranean World*, edited by Anders Klostergaard Petersen and Georg van Kooten, 187–218. Leiden: Brill, 2017.

Laporte, Dominique. *History of Shit*. Translated by Nadia Benabid and Rodolphe el-Khoury. Cambridge, MA: MIT Press, 2002. Originally published in French, 1978.

Largier, Niklaus. *Diogenes der Kyniker: Exempel, Erzählung, Geschichte in Mittelalter und früher Neuzeit. Mit einem Essay zur Figur des Diogenes zwischen Kynismus, Narrentum und postmoderner Kritik*. Tübingen: Max Niemeyer, 1997.

Lerner, Michael. *The Politics of Meaning: Restoring Hope and Possibility in an Age of Cynicism*. New York: Perseus Books, 1997.

Lipovetsky, Mark. *Charms of the Cynical Reason: The Trickster's Transformations in Soviet and Post-Soviet Culture*. Boston: Academic Studies Press, 2011.

Lipovetsky, Mark. "Pussy Riot as the Trickstar." *Apparatus. Film, Media and Digital Cultures in Central and Eastern Europe* 1 (2015). http://www.apparatus journal.net/index.php/apparatus/article/view/5.

Lloyd, Genevieve. *The Man of Reason: "Male" and "Female" in Western Philosophy*. London: Routledge, 1993.

Long, A. A. *Epictetus: A Stoic and Socratic Guide to Life*. Oxford: Oxford University Press, 2002.

Long, A. A. "The Socratic Tradition: Diogenes, Crates, and Hellenistic Ethics." In *The Cynics: The Cynic Movement in Antiquity and Its Legacy*, edited by R. Bracht Branham and Marie-Odile Goulet-Cazé. Berkeley: University of California Press, 1996.

Lucian. "Apology for the 'Salaried Posts in Great Houses.'" Translated by K. Kilburn. In *Lucian*, volume 6, edited by Jeffrey Henderson. Loeb Classical Library. Cambridge, MA: Harvard University Press, 1959.

Lucian. "Demonax." Translated by A. M. Harmon. In *Lucian*, volume 1, edited by Jeffrey Henderson. Loeb Classical Library. Cambridge, MA: Harvard University Press, 1913.

Lucian. "How to Write History." Translated by A. M. Harmon. In *Lucian*, volume 5, edited by Jeffrey Henderson. Loeb Classical Library. Cambridge, MA: Harvard University Press, 1936.

Lucian. "On Salaried Posts in Great Houses." Translated by A. M. Harmon. In *Lucian*, volume 3, edited by Jeffrey Henderson. Loeb Classical Library. Cambridge, MA: Harvard University Press, 1921.

Lucian. "The Passing of Peregrinus." Translated by A. M. Harmon. In *Lucian*, volume 5, edited by Jeffrey Henderson. Loeb Classical Library. Cambridge, MA: Harvard University Press, 1936.

Lucian. "The Runaways." Translated by A. M. Harmon. In *Lucian*, volume 5, edited by Jeffrey Henderson. Loeb Classical Library. Cambridge, MA: Harvard University Press, 1936.

Mack, Burton L. *The Lost Gospel: The Book of Q and Christian Origins*. New York: HarperCollins, 1993.

Mack, Burton L. *A Myth of Innocence: Mark and Christian Origins*. Philadelphia: Fortress Press, 1988.

Marston, John. *The Scourge of Villanie 1599*. Edited by G. B. Harrison. London: Bodley Head, 1925.

Martin, R. P. "The Scythian Accent: Anacharsis and the Cynics." In *The Cynics: The Cynic Movement in Antiquity and Its Legacy*, edited by R. Bracht Branham and Marie-Odile Goulet-Gazé. Berkeley: University of California Press, 1996.

Marx, Karl. "Economic and Philosophical Manuscripts [1844]." Translated by Rodney Livingstone and Gregor Benton. In *Early Writings*. London: Penguin, 1975.

Matton, Sylvain. "Cynicism and Christianity from the Middle ages to the Renaissance." In *The Cynics: The Cynic Movement in Antiquity and Its Legacy*, edited by R. Bracht Branham and Marie-Odile Goulet-Gazé. Berkeley: University of California Press, 1996.

Mazella, David. *The Making of Modern Cynicism*. Charlottesville: University of Virginia Press, 2007.

McIntyre, Lee. *Post-Truth*. Cambridge, MA: MIT Press, 2018.

McRuer, Robert. *Crip Theory: Cultural Signs of Queerness and Disability*. New York: NYU Press, 2006.

Middleton, Christopher, ed. *Selected letters of Friedrich Nietzsche*. Indianapolis, IN: Hackett, 1996.

Moles, John. "'Honestius Quam Ambitiosius'? An Exploration of the Cynic's Attitude to Moral Corruption in His Fellow Men." *Journal of Hellenic Studies* 103 (1983): 103–123.

Morgan, Teresa. *Literate Education in the Hellenistic and Roman Worlds*. Cambridge: Cambridge University Press, 1998.

Mustain, Megan. *Overcoming Cynicism: William James and the Metaphysics of Engagement*. New York: Continuum, 2011.

Navia, Luis. *Diogenes of Sinope: The Man in the Tub*. Westport, CT: Greenwood Press, 1998.

Niehues-Pröbsting, Heinrich. *Der Kynismus des Diogenes und der Begriff des Zynismus*. Munich: Fink, 1979.

Niehues-Pröbsting, Heinrich. "The Modern Reception of Cynicism: Diogenes in the Enlightenment." In *The Cynics: The Cynic Movement in Antiquity and Its Legacy*, edited by R. Bracht Branham and Marie-Odile Goulet-Gazé. Berkeley: University of California Press, 1996.

Nietzsche, Friedrich. "The Anti-Christ." Translated by R. J. Hollingdale. In *Twilight of the Idols and The Anti-Christ*. London: Penguin, 2003. Originally published in German, 1895.

Nietzsche, Friedrich. *Beyond Good and Evil: Prelude to a Philosophy of the Future*. Translated by Marion Faber. Oxford: Oxford University Press, 1998. Originally published in German, 1886.

Nietzsche, Friedrich. *The Birth of Tragedy: Out of the Spirit of Music*. Translated by S. Whiteside. London: Penguin, 2003. Originally published in German, 1872.

Nietzsche, Friedrich. *Ecce Homo: How One Becomes What One Is*. Translated by R. J. Hollingdale. London: Penguin, 2004. Originally published in German, 1908.

Nietzsche, Friedrich. *The Gay Science: With a Prelude in Rhymes and an Appendix of Songs*. Translated by W. Kaufmann. New York: Vintage, 1974. Originally published in German, 1887.

Nietzsche, Friedrich. *Thus Spoke Zarathustra: A Book for Everyone and Nobody*. Translated by G. Parkes. Oxford: Oxford University Press, 2008. Originally published in German, 1883–91.

Nietzsche, Friedrich. *Untimely Meditations*. Translated by R. J. Hollingdale. Cambridge: Cambridge University Press, 1997. Originally published in German, 1873–76.

Nietzsche, Friedrich. "The Wanderer and His Shadow." Translated by R. J. Hollingdale. In *Human, All Too Human*. Cambridge: Cambridge University Press, 1996. Originally published in German, 1880.

Nietzsche, Friedrich. *The Will to Power*. Translated by W. Kaufman and R. J. Hollingdale. New York: Vintage, 1968. Originally published in German, 1906.

Nussbaum, Martha. *Cultivating Humanity: A Classical Defense of Reform in Liberal Education*. Cambridge, MA: Harvard University Press, 1997.

Osborne, Peter. "Disguised as a Dog." *Radical Philosophy* 174 (July–August 2012). https://www.radicalphilosophyarchive.com/article/disguised-as-a-dog.

Plato. "Phaedo." Translated by H. Tredennick and H. Tarrant. In *The Last Days of Socrates*. London: Penguin, 1993.

Porter, J. I. "The Philosophy of Aristo of Chios." In *The Cynics: The Cynic Movement in Antiquity and Its Legacy*, edited by R. Bracht Branham and Marie-Odile Goulet-Gazé. Berkeley: University of California Press, 1996.

Rabelais, François. *The Complete Works of Doctor François Rabelais Abstractor of the Quintessence: Being an Account of the Inestimable Life of the Great Gargantua, and of the Heroic Deeds, Sayings and Marvellous Voyages of His Son the Good Pantagruel*, volume 1. Translated by Sir Thomas Urquhart and Peter Motteux. London: Bodley Head, 1933.

Radin, Paul. *The Trickster: A Study in American Indian Mythology*. New York: Schocken Books, 1972. Originally published 1956.

Rist, J. M. *Stoic Philosophy*. Cambridge: Cambrige University Press, 1969.

Roberts, Hugh. *Dog's Tales: Representations of Ancient Cynicism in French Renaissance Texts*. Amsterdam: Rodopi, 2006.

Romm, James. "Dog Heads and Noble Savages: Cynicism Before the Cynics?" In *The Cynics: The Cynic Movement in Antiquity and Its Legacy*, edited by R. Bracht Branham and Marie-Odile Goulet-Gazé. Berkeley: University of California Press, 1996.

Rose, Arthur. *Literary Cynics: Borges, Beckett, Coetzee*. London: Bloomsbury, 2017.

Rose, Arthur, Robbie Duschinsky, and Jane Macnaughton. "Cynicism as a Strategic Virtue." *Lancet* 389, no. 10070 (2017): 692–693.

Rousseau, Jean-Jacques. *Emile, or On Education*. Translated by A. Bloom. London: Penguin, 1991. Originally published in French, 1762.

Russell, Bertrand. *A History of Western Philosophy*. London: George Allen and Unwin, 1947.

Sade, Marquis de. *Philosophy in the Bedroom*. Translated by Richard Seaver and Austryn Wainhouse. In *The Complete Justine, Philosophy in the Bedroom, and Other Writings*. New York: Grove Press, 1965. Originally published in French, 1795.

Sade, Marquis de. *Juliette*. New York: Grove Press, 1968. Originally published in French, 1797.

Schreier, Benjamin. *The Power of Negative Thinking: Cynicism and the History of Modern American Literature*. Charlottesville: University of Virginia Press, 2009.

Searby, Denis M. "Non-Lucian Sources for Demonax with a New Collection of 'Fragments.'" *Symbolae Osloenses* 83, no. 1 (2008): 120–147.

Seeley, David. "Jesus and the Cynics Revisited." *Journal of Biblical Literature* 116, no. 4 (1997): 704–712.

Seneca. *Letters from a Stoic*. Translated by R. Campbell. London: Penguin, 2004.

Shea, Louisa. *The Cynic Enlightenment: Diogenes in the Salon*. Baltimore: Johns Hopkins University Press, 2010.

Singh, Julietta. *Unthinking Mastery: Dehumanism and Decolonial Entanglements*. Durham, NC: Duke University Press, 2018.

Skoglund, Annika, and Johannes Stripple. "From Climate Skeptic to Climate Cynic." *Critical Policy Studies* (January 2018). doi:10.1080/19460171.2018.1 429938.

Sloterdijk, Peter. *Critique of Cynical Reason*. Translated by M. Eldred. Minneapolis: University of Minnesota Press, 2001. Originally published in German, 1983.

Sparks, Laura. "Re-seeing Abu Ghraib: Cynical Rhetoric as Civic Engagement." *Present Tense: A Journal of Rhetoric in Society* 5, no. 3 (2016). https://www.pre senttensejournal.org/volume-5/re-seeing-abu-ghraib-cynical-rhetoric-as -civic-engagement/.

Stanley, Sharon. *The French Enlightenment and the Emergence of Modern Cynicism*. Cambridge: Cambridge University Press, 2012.

Stanley, Sharon. "Retreat from Politics: The Cynic in Modern Times." *Polity* 39, no. 3 (2007): 384–407.

Steinmüller, Hans, and Susanne Brandtstädter, eds. *Irony, Cynicism and the Chinese State*. London: Routledge, 2016.

Stivers, Richard. *The Culture of Cynicism: American Morality in Decline*. Malden, MA: Blackwell, 1994.

Sussman, Mark. "Cynicism and *The Damnation of Theron Ware*." *Novel: A Forum on Fiction* 47, no. 3 (2014): 403–421.

Taylor, J. D. *Negative Capitalism: Cynicism in the Neoliberal Era*. Winchester: Zero, 2013.

Vaage, Leif E. *Galilean Upstarts: Jesus' First Followers According to Q*. Valley Forge, Pennsylvania: Trinity Press, 1994.

Vaage, Leif E. "Like Dogs Barking: Cynic Parrēsia and Shameless Asceticism." *Semeia* 57 (1992): 25–39.

Vattimo, Gianni. *The End of Modernity: Nihilism and Hermeneutics in Postmodern Culture*. Cambridge: Polity, 2002. Originally published in Italian, 1988.

Virno, Paolo. *A Grammar of the Multitude*. Los Angeles: Semiotext(e), 2004.

Wain, Kenneth. "The Learning Society: Postmodern Politics." *International Journal of Lifelong Education* 19, no. 1 (2000): 36–53.

Walker, Shaun. "Petr Pavlensky: Why I Nailed My Scrotum to Red Square." *Guardian*, February 5, 2014.

Widrich, Mechtild. "The Informative Public of Performance: A Study of Viennese Actionism, 1965–1970." *Drama Review* 57, no. 1 (2013): 137–151.

Wrathall, Mark A. *Heidegger and Unconcealment: Truth, Language and History*. Cambridge: Cambridge University Press, 2011.

Yurchak, Alexei. "The Cynical Reason of Late Socialism: Power, Pretense, and the Anekdot." *Public Culture* 9, no. 2 (1997): 161–188.

Yurchak, Alexei. *Everything Was Forever, Until It Was No More: The Last Soviet Generation*. Princeton: Princeton University Press, 2005.

Žižek, Slavoj. *The Indivisible Remainder: On Schelling and Related Matters*. London: Verso, 2007. Originally published 1996.

Žižek, Slavoj. *The Metastases of Enjoyment: Six Essays on Women and Causality*. London: Verso, 2005.

Žižek, Slavoj. *The Sublime Object of Ideology*. London: Verso, 2008. Originally published 1989.

FURTHER READING

Bracht Branham, R., and Marie-Odile Goulet-Gazé, eds. *The Cynics: The Cynic Movement in Antiquity and Its Legacy*. Berkeley: University of California Press, 1996.

Foucault, Michel. *The Courage of Truth: Lectures at the Collège de France 1983–1984*. Translated by G. Burchell. Basingstoke: Palgrave Macmillan, 2011.

Mazella, David. *The Making of Modern Cynicism*. Charlottesville: University of Virginia Press, 2007.

Shea, Louisa. *The Cynic Enlightenment: Diogenes in the Salon*. Baltimore: Johns Hopkins University Press, 2010.

Sloterdijk, Peter. *Critique of Cynical Reason*. Translated by M. Eldred. Minneapolis: University of Minnesota Press, 2001.

Stanley, Shanon. *The French Enlightenment and the Emergence of Modern Cynicism*. Cambridge: Cambridge University Press, 2012.

Taylor, J. D. *Negative Capitalism: Cynicism in the Neoliberal Era*. Winchester: Zero, 2013.

Yurchak, Alexai. *Everything Was Forever, Until It Was No More: The Last Soviet Generation*. Princeton: Princeton University Press, 2005.

ANSGAR ALLEN is Lecturer in Education at the University of Sheffield and the author of *The Cynical Educator and Benign Violence: Education in and beyond the Age of Reason*.